COLLECTIVE BARGAINING
AND THE
ILLINOIS SCHOOL BOARD MEMBER

plus an extra feature:
Avoid These Pitfalls in Your Teacher Union Contract

Third Edition

Ronald R. Boc

D1072935

ILLINOIS ASSOCIATION OF SCHOOL BOARDS

2921 Baker Drive
Springfield, Illinois 62703-5929

One Imperial Place
1 East 22nd Street, Suite 20
Lombard, Illinois 60148-6120

www.iasb.com

The author

Ronald R. Booth is a labor relations consultant who assists a number of Illinois school boards in their collective bargaining with employee unions. He is a former public school teacher who holds doctorates in both biology (Illinois Institute of Technology) and school administration (Northern Illinois University).

Booth was formerly a staff member with the Illinois Association of School Boards where he served first as a field services director and later as director of management information and executive director of the School Management Foundation of Illinois. He also served as executive director of the North American Association of Educational Negotiators.

Co-author of the first edition of *Collective Bargaining and the School Board Member* in 1978, Booth authored the 1994 revised edition addressing the specific interests of Illinois school board members. He also authored the 2001 updated edition of *Collective Bargaining and the Illinois School Board Member* as well as this third edition in 2009. He co-authored *Planned Appraisal of the Superintendent*, published by IASB in 1976 and now out of print, and has written numerous articles and monographs on school management and labor relations.

COLLECTIVE
BARGAINING
AND THE
ILLINOIS
SCHOOL
BOARD
MEMBER

A practical perspective on
school labor relations reflecting
state laws and local realities in Illinois

The book

Collective Bargaining and the Illinois School Board Member is a special edition of *Collective Bargaining and the School Board Member,* first written by Max A. Bailey and Ronald R. Booth and published by IASB in 1978 and revised by Ronald Booth in 1994.

Collective Bargaining and the Illinois School Board Member combines the revised edition with a thorough examination of state law and local practice in Illinois.

This Third Edition of *Collective Bargaining and the Illinois School Board Member* has been updated by the author and expanded to include an appendix by George M. Kohut on "Avoid These Pitfalls in Your Teacher Union Contract."

The Third Edition also includes an alphabetical index for the first time.

December, 1994
Second edition: July, 2001
Third edition: June, 2009

ISBN: 978-1-880331-24-8

Foreword

When the original version of *Collective Bargaining and the School Board Member* was published in 1978, most school boards were confronting collective bargaining for the first time. Because unionization represented a new phenomenon for school districts everywhere, that little volume found an audience of eager readers among school officials all over the country.

A great deal has changed since then. For one thing, a state law requiring Illinois school boards to recognize employee bargaining units upon demand became effective in 1984. As a result, the proportion of Illinois school boards engaging in teacher bargaining now stands at roughly 98 percent.

Other changes since enactment of the mandatory bargaining law include maturation of the labor-management relationship and increased sophistication of the bargaining process. At least in many districts, parents and taxpayers have grown accustomed to school employee unions. School boards rarely if ever have to deal with the fallout of union organizing.

One thing has not changed, however; it is still imperative for school board members to become familiar with school bargaining and the labor-management relationships in their respective districts. Although most school districts today are engaged in some form of bargaining with their teachers or other employees, newly-elected members of the school board are usually ill-prepared for the pressures that bargaining often creates. Yes, it is true that collective bargaining is a job for well-trained professionals. School boards properly view labor relations as an administrative function and hold their superintendents responsible for effective personnel management. However, the superintendent cannot carry out the negotiations function satisfactorily without clear standards and support from the board.

Moreover, collective bargaining frequently is colored with political overtones in the community. Board members can find themselves under pressure from citizens or employees to answer individually for labor relations problems. Many union leaders, for example, believe they can get more of what they want by isolating the board from its administrative team. Thus, they demand to negotiate directly with school board members.

The more board members know about labor relations concepts, the better they will be able to handle such pressures without compromising the total board or undercutting the administrative staff. Members of the school board must understand collective bargaining, where it fits in the overall scheme of management functions, and the board's proper role in the bargaining process.

That is why this handbook is addressed specifically to school board members. We sincerely hope it will prove helpful as an introduction to school bargaining in all types of situations. In addition, board members should plan to attend bargaining workshops in order to obtain a deeper understanding of the subject.

Further, we believe the article regarding pitfalls in union contracts that appears as Appendix C adds insights essential to responsible school governance. IASB is grateful to George Kohut for providing the article. We also hope the new alphabetical index will add value to the book as a reference source.

Illinois Association of School Boards
June 2009

Contents

(continued)

1. What school board members need to know

When teacher unions began challenging school boards across the country in the 1960s and 1970s, their goal was to establish labor-management relationships patterned after the traditional industrial model that had evolved much earlier in the American private sector. That model begins with the premise that management has the money and power that labor wants. Heavily regulated by federal law, the private-sector model also presumes a protected right of employees to organize and to press management for union recognition. Once recognized as the exclusive bargaining representative of employees, the union uses the threat of impasse and strike to counterbalance management's power at the bargaining table and to gradually extract benefits (money and power) for its membership.

As it did in most industrial states, school bargaining in Illinois grew in the mold of the private-sector model. But the history of school bargaining in Illinois is a history of local options and variations — at least prior to 1984. Up until that year, each school board decided for itself whether to recognize and bargain with local unions. Employee organizations in some districts did not demand bargaining recognition; some did. Among those that did, most eventually obtained the recognition they wanted. Local controversies that erupted over the question of union recognition made the 1970s and early 1980s a very unpleasant time for many school board members, administrators, and teachers as well.

Enactment of a state law requiring school boards to recognize bonafide bargaining units on demand put an end to the recognition disputes. The same law, however, introduced a wide array of other problems for school boards and administrators, and collective bargaining with employees is now a way of life for a big majority of Illinois school employers.

School board members, particularly those new to their positions, may err badly if they prejudge their local labor-management relationship based on the traditional model of collective bargaining as they know it in the private sector. Although labor relations in many school districts across Illinois today fit that traditional model, many do not. All Illinois school districts are subject to the same set of state laws, but differences in local practices and traditions create large variations in the status of labor relations. Some school districts have never reached the traditional model simply because their employees have never demanded it. Still other districts achieved that model, found it wanting, and moved forward to still other variations in their labor relationships.

Labor relations in any particular school district, therefore, may not resemble the industrial model at all.

Due to the numerous possibilities for labor-management relationships among Illinois public schools, it is important for the school board member to learn:

• How does the labor-management relationship work in my district? Is it governed by contract? Does it involve traditional collective bargaining, some other model, or no bargaining at all? What is its history?

• How are school board actions and communications affected by the labor-management relationship? What are the non-bargainable "management rights" and the bargainable "terms and conditions of employment" and how do we distinguish one from the other?

In school districts where employee bargaining units have been established, there will be matters on which the school board cannot act or communicate without union assent. It should go without saying that individual school board members never act or communicate with employees on behalf of the full board unless so authorized by the full board. Where a labor agreement exists, even the full board may not act or communicate with employees on certain specified topics other than through the union. Such topics would typically include wages and working conditions defined as "mandatory subjects of bargaining" by the Illinois Educational Labor Relations Board.

Each school board must understand which topics it may address through policy and which topics must be handled at the bargaining table. Administrators must know which matters they may discuss directly with employees and which topics they must address only with the employees' exclusive bargaining agent.

In addition, school board members and administrators who are confronted with the bargaining process must understand such other matters as:

• the essential distinction between labor relations and human relations;

• how the local bargaining process works and where everyone fits in;

• options available for improving the bargaining process and the pitfalls those options present;

• the major pitfalls contained in some union contract proposals.

These are among the issues that will be addressed in the following chapters.

2. Legal aspects of school bargaining

The right to bargain

The First and Fourteenth Amendments to the U.S. Constitution guarantee to all citizens the rights of association and assembly. These rights provide a constitutional foundation for employees to form organizations and seek recognition from employers. Private sector employees acquired the additional right to bargain collectively with their employers under the National Labor Relations Act (Wagner Act), passed in 1935, and later amended by the Labor Management Relations Act of 1947 (Taft-Hartley Act).

However, the Wagner Act and the Taft-Hartley Act apply only to private sector labor-management relations. Although public employees enjoy the constitutionally protected rights of association and assembly, there is no federal law requiring public employers to bargain collectively with their employees. Rather, public sector employees — including school employees — acquire collective bargaining rights only through state legislation or local employer agreements. Although some states have not bestowed bargaining rights on their public employees, defacto bargaining — or bargaining in the absence of a statutory requirement to do so — was going on in many school districts across America for many years before the states began enacting applicable collective bargaining laws.

Such was the case in Illinois, where employees in many districts acquired the right to bargain collectively by persuading the school board to sit down with the union at the bargaining table and to sign an agreement formally recognizing the union as official bargaining agent. When the General Assembly passed the Illinois Educational Labor Relations Act (IELRA) in 1983, more than half of the school boards in the state were already bargaining with local teachers unions.

Many Illinois school boards resisted pressures to recognize employee unions in the early years of teacher unions. Ultimately, the heated conflicts and strikes over the refusal of school boards to recognize employee unions led to the enactment of the Illinois law, which covers all educational employees and requires school boards to recognize and negotiate with unions that can prove they represent a majority of bargaining unit members.

Illinois law

Some key provisions of the Illinois Educational Labor Relations Act are summarized in *Appendix A,* beginning on page 83. As stated in the Act, the purpose of the IELRA is to "regulate labor relations between educational employers and educational employees, including the designation of employee representatives, negotiation of wages, hours and other conditions of employment and resolution of disputes arising under collective bargaining agreements."

The IELRA also created the Illinois Educational Labor Relations Board (IELRB) and made it the sole administrative body for resolving collective bargaining disputes, representation questions and allegations of unfair labor practices. The Labor Board employs an executive director and a staff of labor relations investigators, attorneys and support staff to gather information, hold hearings and render initial decisions in disputes brought to its attention.

At the first level of consideration, initial decisions in cases are made by IELRB hearing officers and/or the executive director. These decisions are reviewable by the five-member Labor Board upon appeal by one of the parties or on its own motion. Mediation and arbitration functions of the agency also are supervised by the executive director, in conjunction with the Board.

Bargaining agent determination

An Illinois school board confronted for the first time with a union request for formal recognition has two choices: accede to the request and grant voluntary recognition or deny it and force an election among employees. However, a school board may voluntarily recognize a labor organization only upon an affirmative showing that:

• the organization appears to represent a majority of the employees in the bargaining unit;

• there is a basis for the employer's belief that the union represents a majority of employees;

• the bargaining unit involved is an appropriate unit;

• there are no objections or intervening labor organizations, and

• the employer has provided notice to employees of the proposed voluntary recognition and the proposed bargaining unit, along with an affirmative statement that objections may be filed or that parties may intervene.

After investigation, the IELRB can certify the union in question as the exclusive bargaining representative. A secret ballot election becomes necessary when:

• a school board will not voluntarily recognize the union as the exclusive bargaining representative;

• a group of employees no longer wishes to be represented by an exclusive bargaining representative;

• an employer is faced with competing claims between labor organizations that they are the exclusive bargaining representative, or

• the employer has reason to believe that an incumbent union no longer represents the majority of employees in the bargaining unit.

Once properly notified, IELRB staff determines whether the parties will agree to a consent election agreement so that an election may be conducted. If the parties are unable or unwilling to execute a consent election agreement, the matter is set for hearing and a hearing officer issues a Recommended Decision on whether an election shall be held. Unless appealed to the Labor Board, an election is conducted to determine which union, if any, is the exclusive bargaining representative.

Disputes and unfair labor practices

Illinois law also makes the IELRB responsible for:

• mediating collective bargaining disputes where the school board and union are not making adequate progress toward a contract settlement, and

• investigating and ruling on charges that the school board and/or union has committed an act in violation of the IELRA.

To ensure that both school boards and unions bargain in good faith in compliance with the law, the IELRA establishes prohibited activities called "unfair labor practices" (ULP). Either party may file charges against the other for engaging in an unfair labor practice in violation of the Act. When charges are filed, the Labor Board and its agents become hearing officers, a capacity in which they function as judges with the authority to render decisions and judgments against guilty parties.

An unfair labor practice charge (ULP) may be filed by the school board, union or individual employee. Such charges are investigated by a Labor Board agent and a decision rendered by the executive director, who can either dismiss the unfair labor practice charge, a decision which is appealable to the Board, or issue a complaint and set the matter for hearing. The hearing officer may dismiss the charge or find that an unfair labor practice has been committed and order the appropriate remedy. Either decision is appealable to the Labor Board.

The specific actions prohibited by the Act and which constitute unfair labor practices are enumerated in *Appendix A — Some Important Provisions of IELRA,* under the section on

"Unfair Labor Practices" (page 87).

In its rulings, the IELRB interprets and extends the bargaining law to specific circumstances, in effect creating a new body of law on such questions as what must be negotiated and how the parties must conduct themselves. The body of law so created in the years since the IELRB was established in 1984 has a powerful impact on labor-management relations in Illinois school districts. The Labor Board's decisions on ULPS, for example, determine which working conditions are mandatory subjects of bargaining and the meaning of "good faith" under the Act.

Although ULPs are a necessary regulatory mechanism, the manner in which they are defined and enforced can create a legal jungle for school managers. For one thing, if a Labor Board investigator finds that an alleged act has been committed, then the burden of proof shifts from the complainant to the defendant. The defendant is required to show good reason for the act and prove it is not an unfair labor practice.

In some cases, a union may file irrelevant, unwarranted or even frivolous charges in order to pressure the employer to make bargaining concessions. "Give us what we want or we'll file a ULP" becomes a tactical maneuver rather than a means for remedying an illegal act.

Even the most groundless ULP allegations are rarely dismissed prior to investigation by Labor Board staff. Thus, the school district's administrative staff must generate the information necessary to respond to the allegations, a task that can consume substantial amounts of time and legal help. Moreover, even if the matter is dropped before reaching the formal hearing stage, the ULP puts the school board on the defensive by creating a temporary illusion of guilt in the public mind.

School boards and administrators must understand the actions prohibited by the IELRA and take precautions to avoid committing acts that may result in the filing of unfair labor practice charges. Such precautions may not be enough, however, where the filing of ULPs is a part of the union's bargaining strategy.

3: The politics of school bargaining

Initial organizing efforts

School boards typically do not recognize and bargain with employee unions because they want to. They do it because state law requires them to do so upon election by a majority of employees. Historically, emotion has played a big part in the organizing of local employee groups. Union organizing tactics create issues. Emotional issues are often created in order for the union organizer to succeed in getting a majority of teachers or other employees to elect the union to represent them. Once contract bargaining begins, the emotional high is maintained when the high expectations sold to the membership during the organizing campaign produce unrealistic proposals that management cannot accept.

When union recognition is acquired without divisive organizing tactics, as often occurs under Illinois law, the union need not generate a great deal of emotion to obtain employee support. Consequently, and somewhat ironically, the tension necessary for union solidarity must be developed at the bargaining table. The initial victory(s) required for the union to establish credibility with its new members can't come from "winning" recognition as was the case before the IELRA was enacted and, therefore, must come from inflated proposals and protracted adversarial bargaining for the first contract.

The majority of school board members today will probably never be confronted with emotional battles over union recognition, because most Illinois school districts are rather thoroughly organized by unions already. Moreover, where recognition is an issue, the process is carefully regulated by law. However, school board members and administrators in any district may become interested observers of struggles between competing unions, employee efforts to decertify a bargaining representative, or union efforts to organize new employee groups.

Union recognition

Illinois law provides for voluntary recognition, but it is rarely granted because school boards usually want to see the degree of interest shown by employees voting in an election. In a majority of cases, a consent election agreement is hammered out where the key issue is who should be in or out of the bargaining unit. If agreement is not reached and the school board challenges the union's petition, then the IELRB investigates and makes the final decision. This process may become adversarial but the question is resolved in a private, orderly fashion often unnoticed by the rank and file employee.

The school board and administration can play only a limited role in a bargaining unit election. They can be charged with coercion if they threaten to retaliate against the union or its members (such as by unilaterally altering personnel practices or withholding benefits). Nor can management make promises to employees in exchange for votes against the union.

By law the school board may provide employees only with opinions and facts that are not coercive. However, in most bargaining elections, campaign debate occurs *among* the membership and disputes are between employees of differing philosophies, not between the school board and employees.

When a union wins an election, the next step is to prove its worth to the membership by (a) keeping everything employees already have, (b) gaining additional protections and benefits through the collective bargaining process and (c) enforcing the contract through the grievance procedure.

The organized district

The good news is that time typically brings emotional stability as the union becomes more secure in its position and the board-management team becomes more accustomed to the bargaining process. Failure to grow by either side can delay maturation, of course.

The collective bargaining process itself is adversarial in nature. It involves a bilateral power struggle. The only real power that employees bring to bargaining is their services; to demonstrate their power, they will threaten to withhold those services. An adversary relationship does not necessarily lead to intensive conflict, but it does mean that the union will be on one side and management on the other side. Because there are two sides, and only two sides, school board members are management.

In industry, the labor relations process typically pits management (the have's) against labor (the have not's), and it is very easy for the ordinary citizen to side with labor. In public education, however, the underdog is not always labor. Employees often are able to muster much more political clout than management. Even though taxpayers should identify with management quite readily, because it is their money that will pay for the settlement, only school boards are vulnerable to political pressure. Unions are private organizations whose only responsibility is to the vested interests of their membership. They have no responsibility to the public.

Boards members should recognize that some form of collective bargaining was probably always inevitable. When it comes to a particular district, the fact that employees want to negotiate items which were formerly management prerogatives does not mean that the board or superintendent failed. Employees are led to believe that they are second-class citizens if they do not have a contract, and there is not much boards can do to counteract that philosophy.

Thanks to special relationships or other circumstances, union recognition has been avoided or delayed in some school districts in spite of the bargaining law. However, collective bargaining is a way of life for most Illinois school officials.

Another key lesson is that labor peace cannot be purchased. Giving employees what they want today to prevent having to negotiate a formal contract only creates new problems that will have to be faced later. Some of the worst contracts are found in districts that have tried to give benefits away to keep the union away.

To put it simply, teachers have a vested interest in their own employment and want a voice in decisions affecting this employment. Thus, a power struggle develops.

Informal substitutes for bargaining — and the pitfalls

School districts that have avoided formal negotiations probably feel they have kept unions from "taking over the district." Most districts, however, are bargaining with their employees even if there is no signed contract. Meeting and conferring, discussing, communicating, and talking are euphemisms for bargaining in those districts that do not negotiate formally with their employees. Such districts have already begun bargaining without the formality of a signed contract. A lot depends, of course, on what they are talking about. The comfort of informality invariably broadens the scope of issues raised.

School boards that are not engaged in a formal bargaining process probably think they can take care of everything and everyone with board policies. However, these negotiated policies can become a source of difficulties.

Where the board is not confronted with a formal contract, it is easy to confer with teachers about many different topics and issues, including curriculum, board policies, salaries, budgets and district goals. Discussions cover a wide scope of topics, including many that the board would never dream of negotiating in formal bargaining. But this creates what is called "past practice." When these districts are forced to write a contract, they will sit down at the bargaining table and say, "Now that we're going to bargain, we're going to take away all those benefits." That won't work for two reasons. First, now that the union is representing employees at the bargaining table, they cannot afford to lose any previous gains. Second, any neutral third party who may become involved will not grant employees less than what they had before. This is why efforts to buy labor peace eventually cost more than formal bargaining.

Impact of bargaining on board policy making

School boards that engage in formal bargaining also need to use board policies, but not to keep the union away. Boards may bargain many different items relating to the employee-employer relationship, but should continue to establish policies in areas that are beyond the scope of formal bargaining and which do not touch on working conditions. Policies should continue to play an important role in managing the district and in some cases can serve as an alternative to placing something into the contract.

The Illinois Educational Labor Relations Act has severely limited the authority of school boards to make policies governing employees who are organized. Section 4 of the IELRA requires employers "to bargain collectively with regard to policy matters directly affecting wages, hours, and terms and conditions of employment as well as the *impact* thereon upon request by employee representatives." This means that, even if a condition of employment is not addressed in the union contract, the school board cannot change that condition until it bargains the impact with the union.

To further limit the school board's policy making authority, the IELRB has ruled that any change to a working condition must be bargained before action is taken and the impact of that change must be bargained after the action is taken. "Decisional bargaining" requires the Board to anticipate which policy decisions relate to conditions of employment, give proper notice to the union, and bargain in good faith before those policies are changed.

Decisional bargaining is not limited to written board policies. The same rules apply to practices and procedures, both written and unwritten.

In spite of these rules, it is important to remember that board policies and negotiated contracts are separate entities. The distinction between the two must be maintained or boards of education will end up negotiating all of their policies. (Would your board really want the union to help decide when board meetings will be held?)

The union member

In the past, some board members have considered the unionization of teachers and other school employees as inherently evil or non-professional. Out of frustration or inexperience, they blamed themselves or the administration when their teachers turned to unions. In the vast majority of cases, however, the unionization of school employees was far beyond any control of the school board or administration. State law creates powerful pressures for employees to organize, and the political strength of a local union is often abetted by the awesome clout of state and national affiliates.

Moreover, there are a number of social and demographic factors which cause employees to unionize, many of which are beyond the control of local boards and administrators. For example:

• Unions provide a sense of collective power enhanced by the protection of laws and court decisions.

• The size of the school bureaucracy reduces lines of communication. Informal input isn't enough and unionization promises control over individual destinies.

• The increasing age and experience of teachers makes it difficult for the dissatisfied teacher to switch employers. A lack of mobility increases the need for security.

• The teaching profession includes more and more primary family wage earners, while an increasing dependence on two bread winners per family has driven the demand for wage and benefit increases.

• Taxpayers are resentful of increased school costs and demand evidence of results. Reduced funding or enrollment declines may result in layoffs or cutbacks that threaten job security.

• The job of the classroom teacher becomes ever more difficult, thanks to the declining respect for authority, the breakdown of families and rise in at-risk children, and the multi-cultural nature of classrooms across the country.

• Mandates for accountability and the focus on student test scores limit the academic freedom accorded teachers and subject them to continuous scrutiny.

Economic, psychological, and security needs of employees also are factors in their decision to support union strategy and tactics in local situations. The security needs of employees are easily manipulated by skilled union organizers. Even the most benevolent and humanistic school board's reluctance to grant union recognition or to meet contract language and wage demands become tools for the aggressive and skillful union organizer.

Board members find their roles frustrating until they learn to deal with employees both as union members and as human beings. Efforts to give employees more than the union does only intensify union demands. Efforts to break the union only increase tensions and unite employees behind the union.

The board member must distinguish between employee relations and labor relations, so that each can be treated separately, realistically, and professionally. The ability to view the teacher's professional needs as separate and distinct from his or her human (union) needs keeps conflict and frustration to a minimum. Hopefully, this book will be a first step toward acquiring this important ability.

Some changes that bargaining brings

Observers of the collective bargaining scene have identified some changes that the negotiating process typically brings to a school district:

1) Collective bargaining has a leveling effect. The all-for-one and one-for-all concept drives unions to organize and try to get what they want through collective means. Most school managers believe this leveling effect results in mediocrity and it probably does to a certain extent. As policies are amalgamated into a contract and management is forced to treat all employees alike, there is some loss of individuality, creativity, and initiative. In fact, some creative energy is redirected from the classroom to union activities. Union leadership roles are often assumed by creative and gifted teachers. The recognition of their peers offers a stimulus and affords a promotional opportunity not available from management.

2) Individual employee needs are replaced by group needs. This surfaces very quickly when fair share or seniority clauses are brought to the bargaining table. Both of these demands meet the needs of the union organization rather than the individual employee. Unions protect the weak (even the incompetent) to give security to the strong. It is their duty to protect every member in spite of the effect on educational performance.

3) Bargaining statewide tends to equalize differences among districts. Districts in one part of the state will have similar contracts, union goals, and objectives as those in other parts of the state. Local issues will surface but master statewide issues will be predominant.

4) Bargaining creates a new and important management function. It is not something that can be addressed with just the best interests of the district at heart, but requires sophistication and skill. School officials must confront bargaining with a complete understanding of what the process is all about. They must understand the law and the implications of Labor Board decisions. To acquire this understanding, there is no substitute for study and preparation. The management team must be armed with proper skills and relevant information. Adequate preparation and planning make a big difference in how smoothly the process goes, as well as in the final settlement. The results of bargaining will have a greater long term impact than almost all other school board decisions. Trying to get something removed from a contract is much more difficult than keeping it out in the first place.

The nature of school bargaining

Because collective bargaining in the schools has generally evolved in the pattern of the traditional industrial model, it tends to be an adversarial process dependent upon a balance of power. (There are alternatives to the adversarial model, as will be discussed later, but they probably are not appropriate everywhere.) Few argue that the industrial model is ideal for a school district or any other public employer. In fact, it has some serious flaws. Adoption of the model in the public sector is probably due to the fact that it is a known quantity that has generally been successful in the private sector.

The industrial model of labor relations begins with certain assumptions:

1) The employer has the wealth that the union wants for its members and the power that it wants for itself. A union is ostensibly created to serve the needs of employees. But unions, like all organizations, take on lives of their own with goals and agendas that differ from those of both the employer and the employees. A union acquires power by brokering benefits — promising and delivering.

2) In order to be successful in achieving its goals, a union must enjoy a near-equal footing with the employer at the bargaining table. Unless there is a balance of power between board and union, bargaining is a facade. Unions can boast various types of power, including the power to call a strike, the power to take legal action, or the power of political or community pressure.

3) In order to even exist, the union must have the loyalty of employees, or at least a sizeable majority of them.

These conditions are generally as true in the public sector as in the private, but there are some stark differences. In order to acquire an equal footing with the employer, the public employee union must have the weight of law behind it, either by statute or local bargaining agreement. Real union power at the bargaining table, however, usually depends upon the ability to strike — that is, to bring community pressure to bear on the school board through the threat of a strike or to actually go out on strike and stay there until the desired settlement is reached.

Because a successful strike — or a convincing strike threat — depends upon unity or loyalty among union members, unions typically work hard at earning loyalty. In other words, employee unions must continually demonstrate their worth to their members.

A major difference between public sector and private sector unions is in the congruence of their goals with employer goals. In the private sector, the employer must make a profit to continue in business and the union must be careful not to kill the goose that lays the golden eggs — that is, it must not obtain so much wealth and power from the employer that the employer goes out of business. That constraint does not exist in the public sector. Teacher union goals often are not at all congruent with goals of the school board, although the union may make a great public display of its concern for students and quality of education.

It should be noted, however, that mature and secure unions often adopt goals more congruent with those of the board. Immature or insecure unions never do.

Another major difference between the public and private sectors, of course, is that a school district cannot decide to go out of business and cannot routinely pass along increases in labor costs to consumers. Although the economic relationship between employer and employee is much the same in the two sectors, the relationship between employer (school board) and customer (taxpayer) is much different.

Still a third major difference between the public and private sectors is the relationship between owners and customers of school services and between union members and those two constituencies. In the private sector, those people who own the company usually are not the same people who buy the company's products or services. And members of the union are part of neither group.

In the public sector, however, the people who "own" the establishment (taxpayers) are the same people who use its services — and school employees are likely to be part of both constituencies. School employees help elect their own bosses (school board members) and can lead other "owners and customers" to bring powerful pressure to bear on those bosses.

These differences create considerable difficulty with the industrial bargaining model for school boards and administrators.

The political factor

Clearly, what is called "collective bargaining" in the private sector is not necessarily the same thing in the public sector. Because school districts often are saddled with a bargaining process that combines labor relations, human relations and politics, school boards and superintendents find it difficult to represent the public interest and survive professionally. School boards and superintendents regularly survive the process, but the political aspect creates serious difficulties for them.

In its simplest terms, this means that if unions do not get what they want at the bargaining table, board members and superintendents can find themselves in jeopardy. If the politics of impasse or strike doesn't get the superintendent fired, then sometimes it's the loss of school spirit that often follows the strike or the teachers' refusal to maintain acceptable relationships with students and parents.

Even without the rigors of bargaining, superintendents can seal their own doom through neglect of faculty attitudes. Poor communications and other management weaknesses can set employees against both the administration and the board. Today's employees not only talk about their problems out of school, they organize campaigns to unseat board members and to remove the superintendent.

That leaves school boards and superintendents on the horns of this dilemma: How do they protect the public from the unions without making themselves the sacrificial lambs?

Some boards have said, let's forget the public and give the unions what they want. Other boards have stood fast against the union's demands and been ousted at the next election, soon followed to the sidelines by their superintendents.

Clearly, management survival in the face of massive political pressure has to be among management's top objectives in labor relations. Fortunately, many school boards and superintendents have demonstrated that they can indeed achieve the dual objectives of: (a) protecting the public interest at the bargaining table, and (b) protecting themselves against political tactics and the appearance of community support for the union. One answer lies in how management approaches the bargaining process.

The board and superintendent who take union demands as personal insults and who try to beat down the union in the eyes of their employees invariably find themselves in the eye of a storm. On the other hand, those who view bargaining dispassionately and who do their best to understand the needs of both management and labor are most often able to avoid serious conflict. They bargain in good faith but are not afraid to say "no."

The fact remains, however, that board members and superintendents who ignore the political nature of public institutions do so at their own peril. The rest of this handbook explains the respective needs of management and union and shows how board members can deal constructively with unions and their political strategies.

Winning at the bargaining table

School board members must have a clear conception of what "winning" means in a labor relations context.

Does it mean avoiding a strike?

Negotiating the smallest possible salary increase?

Getting some restrictive language out of the contract?

Getting a settlement so school will start on time?

Winning can include any or all of these elements — or none of them, depending upon a lot of factors. One should not judge a labor-management relationship by whether there was a quick settlement or a contract favorable to the board. A quick settlement may be praiseworthy — but reserve your praise until you have looked at the contract. The board may have "given away the store."

A strike may seem reprehensible — but it may have been

an unavoidable union tactic designed to rebuild the unity of its members.

Community pressure that makes the board look good at the expense of the union may lead to premature celebration. An insecure union means more trouble in the future. One thing that winning does not include is making the union look bad.

Once employees have unionized, the board and administration must make up their minds to build stable and unemotional relationships with the unions. The school board's purpose, after all, is a solid educational system, a purpose that cannot be achieved without a stable, productive workforce, effective management and efficient use of resources. Those laudable objectives that guide the board in all its endeavors should also guide its hand in relations with unions.

Therefore, successful collective bargaining can probably be best described as a process in which:

- a contract settlement is reached without a strike;

- contractual agreements are within the board's parameters regarding economic benefit settlements and specific provisions;

- both the board and the union emerge looking good, as though each did its job competently and fairly.

School boards that fill their own roles properly and permit unions to be unions soon find a new equilibrium. A basic understanding of this educational dilemma called "labor relations" will make the realities less threatening and service on the school board less painful.

4. How bargaining works

The Illinois Educational Labor Relations Act defines collective bargaining as "the performance of the mutual obligations of the educational employer and the representative of the educational employees to meet at reasonable times and confer in good faith ... and to execute a written contract incorporating any agreement reached by such obligation, provided such obligation does not compel either party to agree to a proposal or require the making of a concession."

For school boards and superintendents, the bargaining process includes three basic steps: establishing ground rules, initiating proposals, and responding with counterproposals. A fourth step emerging from the first three — determining what will be bargained — is probably the most important step of all.

Ground rules

One of the first steps in the collective bargaining process is the negotiation of ground rules to govern the behavior of both sides. Some ground rules are established by law, of course. Neither side, for example, can determine who will represent the other side. It is an unfair labor practice for the union to insist that the school board not use a consultant or for the board to insist that the union business or Uniserv agent not be present at the bargaining table.

Some statutory procedures can be expanded by contract. Guidelines for impasse and mediation, for instance, are prescribed by law but can be extended by mutual agreement of the parties. Also, the IELRB has ruled that bargaining must occur within 60 days of receiving the demand to bargain but many contracts are more specific. The parties, for example, may agree that bargaining will begin no earlier than and/or no later than a specified date. By design, non-traditional collaborative bargaining processes usually involve restrictive procedures and timelines requiring mutual agreement on more elaborate ground rules.

In general, if by mutual agreement the parties are going to develop procedures different from the norm, then those procedures should be spelled out in detail before negotiations begin. Though each situation is different, the following questions should be answered in the ground rules if not prescribed by law or contract:

1) How often will bargaining sessions be conducted?

2) What should be the length of each session?

3) How many persons will serve on each bargaining team?

4) Will observers be permitted?

5) Will there be joint or separate press releases?

6) Where will sessions be held and at what time?

7) Is an agenda set in advance?

8) If different from law, what procedures and timelines will be followed?

9) Who keeps records and minutes? Are sessions to be tape-recorded?

10) Will there be any guidelines for caucusing?

11) Who is responsible for preparing the final agreement?

These are just some of the questions which need to be answered before the start of contract bargaining.

Initial proposal

By design, bargaining is a game in which the union is always on offense and management plays defense. That is, the union demands to gain what it doesn't have and management tries to retain what it already has. These roles change but rarely. Typical union strategy is to trade two things it does not have for one thing it wants.

Some observers suggest that school boards give too much to the union because they operate from a defensive position.

So people ask, "Why don't school boards take the initiative and make the first proposal rather than counterproposing after the employees make their demands?" The argument seems to make sense on the surface. After all, the best defense is a good offense.

Most experienced negotiators, however, believe that management should not make the first proposal for two reasons. First, the board of education already has what the union wants. Psychologically, it is better for both sides if the board allows the union to make the first proposal. The second reason wise boards don't make the first proposal is that they might propose giving something to employees which the union would not otherwise have thought about.

School boards are free to originate proposals, of course, and they sometimes do when they must try to retrieve something previously bargained away. The retrieval posture is the only time a board has anything to gain from bargaining. It also is a very difficult posture, often impossible.

Boards most likely become aggressors at the bargaining table either when the budget must be cut or when restrictive contract provisions get in the way of sound educational or management practices. However, union negotiators are sure to find such a posture unusual and unsettling and will probably use it to stir unrest among bargaining unit members. Even if the school board has something significant to trade for what it wants, it will probably be something the union thinks it should be getting anyway. Unions deplore giving; their job is getting.

Collective bargaining has been defined as a "zero sum" process in which management gives and labor gets. Unions are uncomfortable with anything else, which makes retrieval bargaining extremely hazardous to labor relations and community relations.

Board's counterproposal

After receiving the initial proposal from the employees, the board's negotiating team should develop a counterproposal to be presented to the union's team at the next bargaining session.

The board team's counterproposal should include items that management wants in the contract, and not be just a reaction to the union's demands. Every counterproposal should be written as an original document, using the board team's language and format. The aim is to get the union negotiator to use the board team's counterproposal as a point of reference. This helps move the contract language toward a management orientation, while minimizing the negative, reactive posture that comes from responding piecemeal to each union proposal. If management is forced to respond and argue every union proposal, then a truly defensive mode is taking place and every change will be perceived as a union loss.

It is not necessary to produce a counterproposal for each item proposed by the union. Deleting specific items which the board team believes to be non-negotiable or unnecessary is not only an acceptable practice but is also good strategy. Initial proposals that do not appear in the board's counterproposal have a chance of being forgotten by the union team. Even deleting items that the board is willing to include is good strategy because it allows the union to win them back.

Analysis of the union's demands is essential. One method is to dissect each section of the proposal and identify: key issues, objectionable language to be avoided at all costs, items which can be agreed to, compromise issues, and management's alterations. The counterproposal can then be developed as a result of the analysis.

Establishing a floor

Management teams bargaining a first union contract typically encounter a new and troubling concept called "past practice." Those bargaining subsequent contracts confront the related concept of "status quo." Both terms reflect the fact that bargaining never begins with a blank sheet of paper.

Past practices: Negotiation of a first contract begins with a foundation based on practices as they currently exist. The concept of past practice can apply to any bargainable subject matter and can tie management to whatever formal or informal practices it may have engaged in prior to the advent of bargaining. Thus, if teachers were permitted to come and go as they pleased during duty-free periods prior to bargaining, it will be assumed that they still have that right under collective bargaining — unless the school board can negotiate a contract clause establishing otherwise. Once a bargaining unit is established, management cannot unilaterally decide to limit teachers' freedom during their duty-free periods. Any effort on the part of management to alter those practices may be treated as a change in "terms and conditions of employment" subject to bargaining.

Status Quo: Under the concept of status quo, the terms, conditions and benefits of an expired contract continue in force until a new contract is agreed upon. Under the Illinois law and Labor Board rulings, if the parties are still negotiating, then the "old" contract terms have to continue. Any change made by the school board prior to mutual agreement on a new contract is considered unilateral action and an unfair labor practice. Thus, unions can prevent takeaways or retrievals by the school board by simply stalling the process and not agreeing to a new contract. The reverse is also true — employees don't get anything new either, but they can stonewall and keep what they had before.

School boards and administrators need to carefully consider past practices and status quo as they develop counterproposals and bargaining strategies.

Good faith bargaining

The law requires that both management and union bargain in good-faith. Failure to do so is an unfair labor practice. "Good-faith bargaining" has a long history of interpretation, giving it a particular meaning in labor law. The following principles of "good faith" have evolved from rulings of courts and the National Labor Relations Board:

1) It is a duty to approach negotiations with an open mind and with a sincere purpose to reach an agreement.

2) The manner and extent of negotiations necessary to satisfy good faith varies from case to case.

3) Long meetings or frequent meetings alone may not be enough to satisfy the requirement.

4) It does not mean that an agreement must be reached; however, if an agreement is reached, it must be reduced to writing at the request of either party.

5) It does not require an employer or the union to agree to a proposal nor make a concession.

The standard used in the private sector to determine whether the parties have bargained in bad faith revolves around one question: Does the bargaining which has taken place indicate that one or both parties came to the negotiations table with no desire to reach a mutual agreement on a contract (i.e. a "closed mind")? Unless a party has absolutely refused to meet with and discuss negotiable issues with the other side, an investigating agency must analyze the entire course of bargaining to determine whether bad faith exists. The difficulty is that no one position can serve as an indicator of bad faith bargaining. The "totality of conduct" approach, as it is called, will involve these observations, among others:

• Did a party refuse to meet at reasonable times to negotiate?

• Did a party seek extensive postponement of meetings?

• Did a party refuse absolutely to discuss the other side's proposals?

It is particularly difficult for school board members to understand that the content, fairness, or reasonableness of their proposal is not an indicator of good faith. In the eyes of the law, it would be bad faith to initially offer a ten percent pay raise and never change the offer, but it would be good faith to offer nothing and increase it to two percent. This concept seems illogical and even ridiculous to those who become impatient and frustrated with the "game" of bargaining.

Boards should be assured that they have the right to maintain positions sincerely held, including "No." In a private sector case tried in federal court, the court noted: "The employer may have either good or bad reasons for insistence on the inclusion or exclusion of a proposed contract term. If the insistence is genuinely and sincerely held, if it is not mere window dressing, it may be obtained forever though it produces a stalemate."

The obligation that a party bargain in good faith does not require the party to make a concession on any specific issue.

If one party makes a demand, the other side is not required to make some movement toward that position. Trade-offs are never required.

The object of both parties at the bargaining table should be to reach a mutually acceptable agreement. Such a goal is not inconsistent with the well-established principle that no party can be forced to concede on a point it believes unacceptable. The appearance of bad faith bargaining increases, naturally, as one party rejects more of the other side's demands outright.

The obligation of the employee organization to bargain in good faith is no different than the obligation of the board to do so.

The obligation of the school board to fairly consider the proposals of the union is no greater than the union's obligation to fairly consider the board's proposals. And boards are not limited to reacting to the demands of the union. Boards may, and should, make initial proposals to change contract terms in order to alleviate unacceptable burdens placed upon them by the current contract or to clarify certain language in the contract. Counterproposals and board demands have a rightful place in the bargaining process.

The absence of good faith on the part of an employer could be inferred from a pattern of conduct, such as: unreasonable fragmentation of bargaining sessions, pointless questioning of the union's proposals, making unnecessarily complicated proposals, making demands outside the scope of collective bargaining, offering less than existing benefits while refusing to grant any benefits over and above those that exist, and unilaterally changing working conditions during bargaining.

What will be bargained?

It is not easy to define the scope of bargaining (that is, what is bargainable?). The standard private sector definition is "wages, hours, and terms and conditions of employment." The problem lies in determining what is meant by "terms and conditions of employment." The definition of what must be bargained upon demand by the union has been gradually expanded by the Illinois Educational Labor Relations Board since it was created in 1984.

The IELRB, by hearing and deciding unfair labor practice charges lodged against school boards that refuse to bargain particular topics, determines which issues are mandatory subjects of bargaining. If an issue is ruled to be a mandatory subject of bargaining, then the parties are required to bargain the subject in good faith.

Good faith bargaining over a mandatory topic does not require agreement on the subject or even contract language. But it does mean the subject cannot be:

a) dismissed unilaterally at the bargaining table, or

b) changed mid-term without notification and bargaining in the case of a change in any policy or procedure not included in the collective bargaining agreement.

Subjects most often negotiable are wages, fringe benefits, hours, employee security, union security, employee discipline, grievance procedures, and methods of employee removal. Items commonly considered exclusive management rights and, therefore, not subject to negotiation typically include institutional mission and program, level of funding, employee hiring, discharge and supervision, job assignment, organization, work force size, service and recruitment standards, and employment conditions for employees who are not part of the bargaining unit.

The negotiability of certain items is subject to interpretation by the IELRB, including parity in wages, class size, pre-eminence of a negotiated contract over existing laws, teacher preparation time, evaluation, reduction-in-force, textbook selection, employee inservice education, and school calendar.

Under current Labor Board decisions, school boards must bargain the impact of decisions that are not in themselves subject to mandatory bargaining (see page 37).

It is probably fair to conclude that the scope of bargainable subjects will continue to expand. School boards are often willing to discuss whatever issues the unions bring to the table. More important, the courts and the IELRB have broadened the definition of "conditions of employment" to cover virtually any topic one might imagine.

Some states have enacted public sector bargaining laws that are more conservatively interpreted and tend to follow more closely the private sector standards of the National Labor Relations Board. Because NLRB rulings give more than lip service to management rights, school boards in those states find they are not required to bargain every imaginable topic. Some state statutes, in fact, narrowly limit the subjects which must be bargained in "good faith" and some even itemize subjects which may not be negotiated.

Other states, like Illinois, rely on unfair labor practice cases to differentiate between mandatory and permissive subjects of bargaining. Here the courts or administrative agencies decide what must be bargained and can expand or shorten the list of bargainable items. In the process, they can clarify or confuse the distinction. They can use or misuse their authority to define scope based on their political or philosophical leanings.

What should be bargained?

What must be bargained will differ greatly from what *should* be bargained and what a school board may be willing to give up at the bargaining table. In spite of the law and Labor Board decisions, the real scope of bargaining is still determined at the negotiating table. The board determines scope on the basis of what subjects it is willing to reduce to writing. **(See Table One.)**

Management negotiators generally agree that the right to hire, transfer, promote, and discipline employees should be

Table One-Typical Teacher Union Demands
(Definitions of many of these terms can be found in the glossary)

Union Demands that Must be Bargained

- Salary schedules
- Extra-duty salary schedules
- Insurance
- Fringe benefits
- Days worked per year
- Grievance procedure ending with arbitration

Union Demands that Must be Bargained but Should be Avoided or Modified

- Hours worked per day
- Preparation time
- Lunch periods
- Retirement bonus/incentives
- Work load
- Leaves — illness, personal, leave of absence, union business, maternity, professional, unpaid
- Class size
- Evaluation procedures
- Employee discipline
- Discharge or termination
- Procedures for reducing work force
- Fair share
- Use of facilities
- Seniority
- Notification of assignments
- Dues deduction
- Transfer and reassignment

Union Demands not Subject to Mandatory Bargaining

- Supervisory duties
- Hiring practices
- Promotion
- Use of emergency days
- Fact finding or interest arbitration
- Academic freedom
- Maintenance of standards (all board policies and past practices)
- Inclusions (e.g. U.S. Constitution, state laws, board policies)
- Discrimination
- Administrator evaluation
- Curriculum and program
- Textbook selection
- Pupil discipline
- Evaluation criteria
- Broad definition of grievance
- Staffing standards: pupil-teacher ratio, etc.
- Professional qualifications
- In-service training
- Citizenship and constitutional protections
- Student teachers
- Committee assignments

treated as non-negotiable. Although these topics usually come up at the bargaining table, management may concede to procedures but should not bargain away the right to make final decisions.

School unions generally hold that anything which affects the employee in any way is negotiable. Unfortunately, the IELRB decisions seem to reflect a similar philosophy. This interpretation is much too broad for management to accept without challenge. School boards in some cases have sought relief in state courts to argue that discretionary powers delegated by the legislature to the school board cannot be diminished by a contract. Although the courts are reluctant to override the IELRB, they have reversed some decisions which have strayed far away from conventional wisdom and/or common sense.

In general, the goal of management is to limit the scope of bargaining as much as possible for at least two reasons. First, education is a public function. The public's elected representatives must have final authority over the schools, including final authority in hiring, transferring, promoting, and disciplining employees. A second reason for limiting the scope as much as possible is primarily a practical consideration. For boards of education, the bargaining process sometimes boils down to an effort to limit the scope as much as possible this year so there will be something to negotiate next year. The bargaining process for boards of education has become one of slowly bargaining away many of the decision-making powers which were formerly exercised unilaterally. Because unions will always need to win in negotiations to satisfy members, a gradual process of concessions will allow for wins but keep the simple contract from escalating into an exhaustive document.

The goal of teacher unions in contract bargaining, in general, has been to expand the scope of bargaining as much as possible and to include by reference such items as board policies, state and federal laws, and state and federal constitutions. Usually these items are offered as harmless verbiage that seems innocent enough. However, their inclusion will eventually lead to trouble. Although a school board is required to uphold both constitutional and statutory law, incorporating these laws in the negotiated contract puts the school board at double jeopardy by making state and federal laws grievable under the contract as well as actionable in court or before government agencies. Including school board policies in the contract tends to destroy a very important power of the board — the authority and responsibility to adopt policy governing the management of the district.

For more insights into the problems created by certain union contract proposals, see Appendix C, "Avoid These Pitfalls in Your Teacher Union Contract," by George M. Kohut.

Contract vs. policy

There are important distinctions between board policies and the negotiated contract. Board policies may be researched and developed through a democratic process, and formal adoption can be accomplished only by vote of the school board at a public meeting. The negotiated contract, by the very nature of the bargaining process, is a bilateral agreement privately arrived at. When negotiated contracts include all policies (even if only by reference), the distinction between policies and contract is gone. Future boards of education may be unable to alter policies except through negotiations with the union.

In order to grasp the distinction between policies and contracts, it's helpful to understand their respective characteristics. Board policies are usually broad statements of intent which allow administrators to select the best ways of carrying out the board's wishes. Negotiated contracts, on the other hand, should contain explicit language that allows little flexibility in implementation and little room for error in interpretation.

Because board policies guide all operations of the school district, they are heavily influenced by federal and state laws and regulations as well as rulings handed down by federal and state courts. More important from the standpoint of local control, school boards are obligated to reflect community values and needs in the development of policy. Board policies generally provide administrators with considerable latitude in making day-to-day decisions.

A negotiated contract, on the other hand, creates specific requirements and limitations in those areas of district operations relating to employees. The contract becomes part of the law that regulates the school board and administration. Ambiguities in the contract are not usually advantageous for the board of education and should, therefore, be avoided as much as possible. Broad philosophical statements should not be included in the contract, because they become subject to interpretation through the grievance procedure. Administrators should interpret the contract literally.

Although the school board may try to withstand union pressure to negotiate board policy items, experience shows that some will probably creep into the negotiated contract. When this happens, the contract item supersedes board policy and any attempt to keep that item as a separate policy statement is an exercise in futility. The policy handbook should no longer contain the written policy in its former spot, but should refer to the appropriate section of the negotiated contract. Attaching the contract as an addition to the policy handbook seems to be an appropriate step to take as more and more policies are pre-empted by the negotiated agreement.

Even though there is almost a fatalistic recognition that negotiated contracts will continue to include more and more items which were formerly board policy matters, the board of education should continue to exercise the right to adopt appropriate policies. Individual contract items will continue to supersede individual board policies, but in policy areas untouched by the contract school boards usually retain the authority and the responsibility to adopt policies which have the force of law in the operation of the school district. They can lose that right by agreeing to broadly incorporate or include the policy manual in either the contract or the grievance procedure.

Impact and mid-term bargaining

Collective bargaining is typically perceived as a periodic process of contract revision or renewal. That is, sometime before the current contract expires, negotiators for the school board and the union sit down to bargain a new contract or changes to the old one. And that may be all the process involves in states without bargaining laws.

In Illinois, school boards are required to bargain with employee unions over terms and conditions of employment and changes in those terms do not always occur in the successor contract bargaining cycle.

Mid-term bargaining (or interim bargaining) becomes a factor when school management decides to take an action during the term of a contract when that action involves a matter deemed a mandatory subject which is negotiable under the law. The action may be in response to a new state law or to a budget crisis or simply a desire of the board to do something different. Examples might include altering class sizes, reducing staff, extending the school day, scheduling parent-teacher conferences after school hours, or eliminating a program or course of study.

Because any board or administrative decision may involve a negotiable matter, some school districts find themselves engaged almost continuously in bargaining some issue or another even though a valid contract is currently in force. If a management decision has an impact upon a mandatory subject that — by law or contract — must be bargained, the school board will have to notify and bargain with the union *before* the decision can be made or implemented if the union demands to do so. This is termed "decisional" bargaining.

The IELRB has ruled that good faith bargaining requires 60 days or more. This means that the union must be notified of a proposed change more than 60 days before the change is acted upon. Further, once the decision is made, the board may have to bargain the decision's impact on other terms and conditions of employment. Even if the decision is purely an inherent managerial right that does not require decisional bargaining, the impact of that decision may have to be bargained.

Mid-term bargaining can be avoided if the union contract contains a strong zipper clause. A zipper clause functions as a waiver of union bargaining rights during the term of the contract, and is obviously an important clause for the school board to get in the contract. Even when the law itself does not subject an issue to bargaining, a school board may be required to bargain the issue mid term if its current contract makes that issue negotiable and contains no zipper clause.

Impact bargaining arises because the IELRA requires the school board to bargain the impact of any management decision that affects terms and conditions of employment. Impact bargaining should be distinguished from "decisional bargaining," another type of mid-term bargaining that involves bargaining with the union before implementing a change in some mandatory subject of bargaining. In contrast, if a management decision does not involve a mandatory subject of bargaining, the board is free to make an unfettered decision; however, the board must bargain the effect that decision has on employees if the union asks to do so (impact bargaining).

In bargaining the impact of a managerial decision, the school board must entertain union proposals aimed at softening that impact. In a staff reduction, for example, the union might propose severance pay or continuation of certain fringe benefits. The school board, of course, is under no obligation to accept any of these proposals. In fact, it is generally accepted that board negotiators must continue to bargain impact until both sides agree they have reached impasse or the legal requirements for impasse have been met.

It is assumed that the school board's final position can be imposed if impact bargaining has not led to an agreement and impasse has been reached. However, the IELRA does not define the specific standards for impasse and unions do not want to admit that there is any point at which management may impose its last position. Unions take the position that bargaining should continue ad infinitum until agreement is reached, an idealistic and improbable definition. Because operation of the school district must go forward, bargaining forever is impractical and boards must rely on conventional labor law for a standard.

Impasse standards are behavioral as well as procedural. In general, impasse occurs when neither party is willing to make further proposals or concessions, sufficient time and/or meetings have occurred, and the parties have bargained in good faith. *For more about "impasse," see Chapter 9, Disputes.*

The more broadly the statute and Labor Board decisions define "terms and conditions of employment," the wider the range of board and administrative decisions subjected to both mid-term and impact bargaining. Further, a school board may be required to bargain both a decision and its impact. For example, the Illinois Educational Labor Relations Board has held that a staff reduction is a mandatory subject requiring 60 days of decisional bargaining and — in addition — that a school board must bargain the impact of any such reduction on terms and conditions of employment. Therefore, while a school board is authorized by law to reduce staff, it must first bargain the decision and then bargain the impact of that decision if the union makes a timely demand to do so.

Impact bargaining and even some decisional bargaining becomes a ritual that board negotiators must go through with little by way of practical outcome. Rarely can union officials give their blessing to any staff reduction, for example, so there is truly no room for negotiation, compromise or concessions over the decision. And in most mid-term negotiations, without the possibility of a strike, the union has very little bargaining leverage. Mid-term bargaining, therefore, becomes a political battle and a test of endurance. However, both decisional and impact bargaining require good faith efforts to resolve differences and need to be taken seriously by the school board and administrative team.

5. Alternative bargaining styles

As noted earlier, collective bargaining is traditionally a bilateral adversary process involving two different and conflicting sets of goals and aspirations. Through negotiations, the two parties attempt to accommodate their divergent goals, a process that works best in an atmosphere of mutual understanding and respect. When the process degenerates into personal rancor, threats and work stoppages, both sides lose.

Dissatisfaction with the traditional adversary bargaining model has prompted a growing number of school boards and unions to experiment with other ways of reaching accord. Some of these non-traditional approaches are worthy of emulation, some are not. All depend upon local circumstances for their success.

In today's public school environment, chances are good that the labor-management relationship in most school districts falls somewhere between the extremes of traditional and non-traditional bargaining. The school board member needs to be familiar with the full range of possibilities, because the bargaining relationship is usually in a constant state of moving toward one extreme or the other.

The traditional approach

The basic purpose of traditional bargaining is to remove power and authority from one party (management) and transfer it to the other party (the union). The vehicle is the contract, or negotiated agreement. Compromise and concession form the style in adversary bargaining, based on demands from the union and counterproposals from management.

The process works while lines of communication are open. But rancor between management and employees typically leads to bargaining through the news media and other forms of open and public dispute. The union strives to get public support on its side; the school board follows suit. Both sides lose and the school district as an educational institution suffers the consequences.

Unfortunately, public sector unions have with few exceptions adopted this private sector model.

In early stages of a bargaining relationship, some educators find the traditional adversary model distasteful and attempt to circumvent its realities. While some have found success in avoidance strategies, others have courted disaster resulting in huge union gains.

It is essential to understand that if the end product is a contract, then the process is collective bargaining regardless of what you choose to call it. Describing the bargaining process as a "forum for communications and cooperative problem solving," for example, often disguises the fact that real conflict exists. Such a description appeals to many educators and school board members who place a high value on cooperation and communication. However, cooperative decision making involves just one side — a team. In bargaining, there are two sides. Consequently, the terms "cooperation" and "bargaining" are contradictory if not mutually exclusive.

In a few Illinois school districts, decisions are still made through cooperative non-bargaining processes. In most districts, however, decisions are made through bargaining. Once employees unionize and demand a contract, some form of bargaining is obligatory.

Traditional bargaining doesn't have to be adversary in its most negative connotation, however. All of us engage in adversarial bargaining in our everyday lives when we buy cars and other commodities. We negotiate daily with colleagues and family members. We accommodate, compromise and concede in many activities.

Many, if not most, collective bargaining agreements are hammered out without impasse, strike, and hostility. Many bargaining issues can be resolved through integrative (problem solving) approaches. Other issues (such as wages) are usually resolved at the other end of the continuum — the distributive or rigid offer-counteroffer approach. In between are packaging and trading approaches. If the objective of *both* parties is to reach an acceptable agreement with the least amount of conflict, then resolution of most issues can be accomplished in a non-distributive fashion. Experienced negotiators prefer to take a non-confrontational approach and avoid distributive behavior as much as possible — at least to a point when final positions are too far apart for resolution and impasse procedures are required.

Skilled negotiators understand that one can disagree without being disagreeable and that agreements can be reached without resorting to antagonism, badgering, and personal attacks. As bargaining relationships mature, negotiators on both sides find a greater degree of comfort with problem solving.

Non-traditional efforts

The usual outcome of traditional bargaining is that both sides lose a little. In an earlier section it was suggested that negotiating from a board perspective is a gradual process of losing as little as possible. Unions also feel a sense of loss because they don't get as much as they want. Rarely do both sides feel winners unless they both gain something very important that overshadows their losses.

Those are both acceptable results with long range benefits to the institution. If one party wins and the other obviously loses, then there will probably be a "get even" mentality from the loser, creating strife and conflict in future negotiations. If union members feel that they didn't get a fair settlement or if their leadership wants greater support or recognition, then their leadership becomes aggressive and confrontational, creating hostility and impasse. If management feels they have been "had," then they become rigid, regressive, and draw firm positions creating confrontation.

Most people want to avoid strife. Those in the political and public arena of education find that labor relations strife often conflicts with other goals, e.g. re-election, tax referenda, job security, and educational improvement. As a result, educators have long sought ways to avoid the political pressures of impasse and conflict that come with collective bargaining.

Districts with a continuing history of conflict have been most active in seeking alternatives to public displays of power. In those districts, the survival of both individual careers and the educational mission of the schools depends on finding an alternative to restore credibility with the public.

Moreover, the movement toward teacher empowerment as part of educational reform has re-fueled interest in non-traditional bargaining. Participative management and/or shared governance has been recycled as site-based or building-level management and integrated into the labor-management mix. Advocates claim that involvement in building decisions (including economics) increases communication, provides a vehicle for collaboration on the real mission of the school, and neutralizes the "we-them" concept of negotiations.

Skeptics argue that site-based management is a union ploy to gain control at the building level. As evidence they cite the union's unwillingness to relax contractual limitations on management and its insistence upon right of approval for any contract waivers or exceptions.

Whether site-based decision making is either or neither of the above, it has gained popularity among reformers and school officials. Some states have mandated site-based models. If collaboration is working effectively in the site-based model, then that changing relationship and attitude should make collaborative labor relations at the district level more attractive to both management and the union.

There have been some encouraging trends toward collegial, non-adversary bargaining models. Some districts have been successful in finding processes that concentrate on integrative approaches while minimizing the distributive nature of the process. Success, if defined as an acceptable contract without conflict, has occurred when both parties agree that the old way wasn't successful and develop mutual ownership in a new process or procedure.

The importance of joint ownership in a new process can't be overstated because *any* process can succeed if all participants share the procedural and behavioral goals to succeed. If only the board or only the union desires change, then any process is doomed to failure.

(The fact that the union supports the traditional model while management does not probably explains most failures of alternative models!)

Process is certainly important in the public sector because how school officials are viewed by their constituents is often more important than what they do. Perceptions are often more important than truth or facts. Boards as political/public bodies need to look good. They want to avoid confrontation. Likewise, farsighted unions have come to recognize that economic gains depend upon public support and funding.

School managers also have other responsibilities and obligations. A collective bargaining contract has a great deal to do with the public's interest in good schools and the rights of students and parents. Therefore, in spite of the obvious advantages of non-traditional processes, school managers must approach such alternatives with caution. The product of any collective bargaining process is a contract. This product (contract) is the *most* important outcome of negotiating, because it affects the institution for a long time (maybe forever). Retrieving losses requires a long recovery period and is rarely collaborative.

Unions also share the goal of a good contract. But their time frame for recovering losses (or no gains) extends only to the expiration of the contract when they can again seek what they lost (or didn't get) in the last round of negotiating — a very short recovery period.

Win-win negotiations

Attempts to find alternative processes began in earnest in the early 1980s. A number of processes emerged, but the most popular was developed by a sociologist whose forte was conflict resolution and hostage intervention, not labor relations. Irving Goldaber created and promoted a model called "win-

win," a program successfully marketed and copied throughout the nation. Win-win is a highly structured and elaborate set of ground rules that requires joint ownership and acceptance of certain restrictions (protocols). The win-win model in its most restrictive form involves:

• Approval by the leadership of both parties and formal agreement to the protocols prior to beginning (to create ownership of ground rules).

• Agreement that personal goals are of less value than the survival and needs of the institution.

• A neutral facilitator to oversee the joint session and enforce protocols.

• All members of the board and the superintendent participate with union representatives in joint, marathon weekend sessions attended by all team members, who are arranged in a circle of chairs rather than across a traditional bargaining table.

• The teams are of equal numbers and usually large (10 to 15 people each).

• Subcommittees are formed to deal with issues (negotiate between joint sessions).

• A commitment to reach closure at the end of the pre-established final weekend.

Many variations of the win-win model have surfaced, some using portions of win-win as alterations to a more traditional approach. For example, the initial joint session where information, ideas and concerns are shared openly has been used to open lines of communications prior to more traditional bargaining. It serves as preliminary sensitivity training for the parties and puts participants in a positive frame of mind.

Interest-Based Bargaining, also called "Integrative Bargaining," is a popular variation of the win-win philosophy. Here the parties strive to identify their respective basic interests in the hope that those interests might be served without serious detriment to either party.

Expedited bargaining

The restricted time frame of win-win also has found favor with both traditional and non-traditional proponents. A process called "expedited bargaining" adopts the marathon bargaining sessions and predetermined closure time of win-win to replace the multitude of briefer sessions typical of traditional bargaining. Expedited bargaining may or may not involve other components of win-win.

Although the restricted time frame of win-win and expedited bargaining reduces the number of meetings, the total time spent may be equal to or greater than in traditional bargaining.

Other variations of the collaborative theme have been developed. Unfortunately some border on hucksterism and, at best, are commercializations created by entrepreneurs. The majority, however, are the offspring of win-win bargaining and are designed to provide a more collaborative environment. Some labels that have been used include: integrative bargaining, cooperative bargaining, dual concept bargaining, conceptual bargaining and process bargaining.

Common to most of these models are the following:

- Broader team membership
- Reduced reliance on a single spokesperson
- A restrictive time frame
- A firmly established time for closure
- Some form of non-confrontational interaction
- Emphasis on problems and solutions rather than positions
- Apparently open and honest communications
- Ongoing year-round problem solving

Evaluating the possibilities

Before embarking on a cooperative approach to negotiations, the school board and administration must be able to give a resounding "yes" to the following question:

Do we have the skill, ability and experience to exercise the same level of control over the outcome (contract) as we do in the current bargaining process?

If the answer is no or we don't know, then it would be wise to reject a non-traditional process — or to first take steps to acquire the skills essential for success.

School managers and school boards should not agree to trade a more amiable relationship or procedure for contract gains. The public interest demands that they not trade a bad product for a good process. On the other hand, if a school board has a history of confrontation and finds a real desire by the union to share ownership in the new process, then a non-traditional approach may be advantageous.

Keep in mind that a union does not waive its rights under IELRA by agreeing to an alternative bargaining procedure. If the alternative model does not produce an agreement, then the union can still seek resolution through the procedures established for impasse, including mediation and the right to strike.

Collaborative bargaining may be a possibility in your district. But do not jump at it because it sounds good, is in vogue or worked well somewhere else. The decision to alter your bargaining relationship should be considered carefully and cautiously. If both process and product can be improved, of course, the organization will be ahead. But if process replaces product, then one problem is converted to another, perhaps more serious, problem.

6. The human element

The board's reaction

Boards of education take their responsibilities seriously. Many boards viewed it as a challenge to their authority when employees — teachers, in particular — first demanded union recognition. Some board members still today take offense when the union presents unreasonable demands at the bargaining table. Board members wonder why and are unsure of how to respond.

One response is to try to buy peace by giving employees what they want, hoping that the demands once met will go away. Another is to pretend to bargain. Other boards may respond aggressively, trying to demean the opposition and destroy the union.

None of these responses is realistic. First, there isn't enough money available to prevent unionization. Labor peace cannot be purchased. Teachers and other employees, propagandized by unions, believe they are second-class citizens if they don't have a contract as good as others. Reacting with aggression or pretending to bargain by simply going through the motions only creates resentment and further strife and may even involve IELRA violations (unfair labor practices).

Stalling tactics often create problems in non-bargaining districts that surface when the board finally agrees to bargain. For example, a board's past practices serve as the starting point for bargaining. Boards that give and give to reduce the demand for a written contract find they can't take back what they have already given when they finally are forced to negotiate. Such boards have little left to bargain with.

A more appropriate response for school boards is to recognize that collective bargaining with unions is a fact of life and to prepare by becoming more sophisticated and more skilled in dealing with organized employees.

Boards of education must recognize that the union — not the board — is going to represent employees. Although reluctant to give up its authority, the bargaining school board can no longer say that these are "our teachers" where terms and conditions of employment are concerned. Boards represent the management viewpoint for those issues that are negotiated. They have to recognize that when something is given to employees, the union gets the credit — not the board. If the union does not get the credit, it looks bad in the eyes of its members. And that is going to create problems, because union leaders must have the support of their members (including dues).

Successful school boards allow the union to win for their workers about what they would have gotten anyhow, but they let the union take the credit. That's successful bargaining from a management point of view, even though it destroys the concept of the school board doing good things for teachers and students. In the eyes of the teachers, the union is going to get credit for all the work done by the board, and the board will have only the privilege of going to the taxpayers to obtain the funds necessary to finance the negotiated package. School boards and administrators then confront the reality that they must manage by policy and contract. This reality comes etched in stone — a policy can be changed anytime by a school board vote; a contract can be changed only with union consent or by a court of law. At the bargaining table, boards of education should try to retain their authority and their options in decision making, but the issues on which they can make unilateral decisions become fewer in number each year.

Constraints on bargaining

What do teacher unions want? In general, they must pursue all they can get. To justify its existence and retain the allegiance of its members, the union must get more each year. How much more will depend on the expectations of the membership.

Common union objectives include more economic benefits,

more security, and more power. In the absence of bargaining, all of these items are determined by unilateral action of the school board. Therefore, anything the union can get is more than they started with. In many cases, as long as they obtain more each year, the members believe that the union has done a good job.

School board members new to collective bargaining need to recognize the basic differences between the public sector and the private sector. Some of those differences are presented in **Table Two.**

Human relations and labor relations

School managers often confuse human relations with labor relations. Their thinking is that "maybe if we deal on a human level the need for a union will disappear." Humanistic board members and administrators are easily confused by the distinction between human relations and labor relations. They try to make human relations programs replace labor relations even though the two are distinctly different, incompatible, and serve different purposes. Basic differences between labor relations and human relations are listed in **Table Three.**

Humanistic managers who "play" bargain typically produce a terrible contract covering everything imaginable, unheard of benefits, and a vocal, successful and domineering union. Human relationships in the schools will not necessarily be improved — people will not have grown and developed or the district's goals met. Bargaining can't supplant human relations efforts any more than human relations programs can resolve labor relations disputes. Only the union organization itself grows fat and healthy when management is naive and gratuitous.

When management finally discovers what it has done and tries to recoup its losses, open warfare develops. Then both labor relations and human relations suffer, a situation that could have been avoided if the two processes had been treated separately from the beginning.

Table Two — Private Sector vs. Public Sector

Private Sector Company	Public School
1) Selects its target populations for marketing products.	1) Must accept clients who live within the district boundaries.
2) Prices can be increased by management.	2) Citizens vote on most tax increases.
3) Can change its location, seeking more favorable work force.	3) School district can't move.
4) Can go out of business if unable to meet union demands.	4) School district stays in business no matter what happens (almost).
5) Can share profits with workers.	5) Schools have no profits to share.
6) Customers select and pay for the products or services they want.	6) All citizens pay for school services, whether or not they use them.

Table Three — Human Relations and Labor Relations

	Human Relations	Labor Relations
Process	Consensus	Adversary
Agenda	Problems and Needs	Demands
Arena	Personal-Humanistic	Legal
Result	Change or Development	Contract Obligation
Emphasis	Self-actualization and Growth	Economics and Security
Goals	Internal (for the school)	External (for the union)
Participants	Individuals	Union
Location	Local Issues	Statewide Demands
Benefits	To organizational goals and clients through better programs	To union and its members through increased benefits, power, security

The importance of credibility

Credibility is the tie that binds school board and community. Regardless of any differences of opinion that might separate a board and community, real problems do not begin until the community decides that the board isn't being honest.

The difficulty presented by some teacher union leaders is that, even if they know the board is telling the complete truth, they may still try to destroy the board if it's in their best interest to do so. The union leader, as distinguished from the rank-and-file teacher, is more than an adversary across the bargaining table; by job description he's an adversary, period. Organizing a union is a political process, and part of the organizer's job is to destroy the credibility of management. Loss of credibility usually means loss of job effectiveness and, maybe, loss of job. Even with mature unions, credibility attacks are part of the strategy at impasse, particularly if a strike occurs.

Managers in the private sector understand this and go to some pains to ensure that boards of directors and shareholders get the management viewpoint when workers strike. The management of General Motors may not have much credibility with employees when it comes to bargaining issues, but they surely have credibility with company owners. Private sector managers are rarely fired because of what employees say or do.

In the public sector, the public is the owner and employees are a part of the public-owner group. The shareholders (taxpayers) have diverse interests. Parents may believe the board should give teachers whatever they want in order to keep them satisfied and keep schools open. Older residents or large property owners, in contrast, may say, "give them nothing and make it retroactive." An economic interest is only one of many variables when citizens choose sides. Having kids in school for babysitting reasons is a very powerful economic motive for parents to apply pressure on school boards regardless of whom they support on the issues.

Building credibility

For a school district, good community relations begin with good staff relations. Teachers and other employees are regarded by their friends and neighbors as experts on all school matters. Research shows that custodians have more ready listeners than do principals or superintendents. If teachers and custodians are to serve as ambassadors of goodwill, boards must see that they have all the facts. When the community gets different versions from administrators and teachers, it's a rare superintendent who can marshal more public support than can the combined efforts of the faculty.

Superintendent survival, therefore, may depend upon employee attitudes as much as upon the school board. If that's the case, what can the superintendent do about it? What can the board do to protect the superintendent?

The same answer comes back again: Establish and maintain credibility. The superintendent who tries too hard to make teachers like him will fail, because people can love — but not respect — someone they can push around. The one who views teachers as enemies will also fail.

Teacher militancy and unionism force school managers to balance benefits for constituents (students and taxpayers) with benefits for employees. In the past, the shrewd administrator could play both ends against the middle, devising a school budget according to the superintendent's priorities and still keeping everyone relatively happy. That isn't so easy when teachers begin talking in negative terms to friends in the community or fighting for "a piece of the action."

Credibility today depends upon effective, action-oriented administration and communications that correspond accurately to the facts. If school boards aren't going to give teachers a share in decision making, they must say so and mean it! If they are, they must plan carefully, do it well, and mean it!

Credibility for the board and superintendent alike boils down to this:

Know what you mean;

Say what you mean;

Mean what you say.

7. Preparing to bargain

Bargaining preparation is crucial. Over the past two decades, teacher unions have made substantial inroads into school board power and authority largely because of their superior preparation. For board members, adequate preparation for bargaining includes acquiring knowledge about unions, selection of a negotiating team, and pre-bargaining planning.

Union preparation

The superior preparation of unions is widely recognized and can be attributed to at least two factors. First, employee organizations generally enjoy more continuity of leadership than boards do. Some employees get deeply involved in union leadership and bargaining. This involvement becomes almost a second job.

School boards also get extensively involved in bargaining. However, board members do not serve on boards for as long as teachers serve as teachers. In some school districts, a board member's tenure is roughly equivalent to the amount of time required for a teacher to acquire tenure.

A second factor is that unions have money and staff. Superior financial resources play a big role in providing unions with special advantages over school employers. Unions can purchase expert training and counseling, as well as the services of experienced negotiators. Union dues are substantial and provide at-the-table negotiators, attorneys, and research services not available to local school boards. Boards should understand that this union expertise is at their negotiating table even if not physically present.

Unit determination

The IELRA prescribes the selection of an exclusive bargaining representative step-by-step (see page 6). Even though statutes supposedly cover the question, challenges to who will be included in the bargaining unit is one continuing source of conflict. The primary arguments center on management and/or supervisory personnel, short-term employees and confidential employees. While there is general agreement that supervisors and confidential employees should be excluded from rank-and-file employee bargaining units, there is considerable disagreement about which specific jobs fall into these categories.

The Illinois Association of School Boards in 1983 identified management and supervisory positions as those which require their incumbents, among other things, to act or recommend action on behalf of the school board with respect to any of the following: hiring, assigning, transferring, promoting, evaluating, rehiring, or failing to rehire, laying off or recalling, or disciplining of any employee or implementation or administration of the collective agreement at any level in the organization or adjustment of grievances at any level. Confidential employees are those who are privy to the employer's labor relations information or strategy. These definitions mirror the state statute, although the IELRA also requires that a preponderance (at least 50 percent) of an individual's time be spent in those activities in order to be exempt from the bargaining unit.

Disputes arising over bargaining unit determination are channeled through the Labor Board and, if necessary, through the courts. Sometimes it's simpler to negotiate the issue with the union in exchange for consenting to the election.

Selecting the negotiating team

As union and school board prepare for bargaining, each side must select a negotiating team. This decision is critical because interaction between the two teams influences the outcome of bargaining.

In general, the board of education should not get involved in the selection of the union negotiating team. (Such involvement is an unfair labor practice.) Unions, of course, would be well-advised to select representatives who are competent and who have the authority and credibility to negotiate for the unit. Management representatives appreciate competency on the opposing side of the table because it facilitates the bargaining process.

There is considerable disagreement among management negotiators as to what constitutes an ideal negotiating team. Composition of board teams varies all the way from board members only to administrators only. One fact is certain: An ideal team in one situation may not be an ideal team in other situations. Each board of education should assess its own bargaining environment and then choose the team which will work best.

A difficult question is whether board members should serve on the team. Bargaining is certainly an administrative activity and policy setters are cautioned not to administer. However, the presence of a board member may bring some credibility to the table and in some smaller districts board members may be the only people available who are not part of the faculty bargaining unit. If board members are willing to spend the time and accept the political ramifications, then they can be a valuable source of credibility, especially in communicating back to the full board.

Negotiating teams should contain at least three persons but ideally not more than five. Fewer than three limits the ability of the team to relate to various aspects of the district's operation. More than five team members may be cumbersome.

Selecting the chief negotiator

Selection of the chief negotiator is probably the single most important decision to be made regarding the composition of the management negotiating team.

Who should serve as the chief negotiator? Although there are varying opinions, most authorities agree that neither the superintendent nor any of the board members should serve as the chief negotiator. An outside professional or a central office administrator probably should fill this important role. Whoever is selected should be skilled or should receive extensive training. It is imperative that the chief negotiator know and keep abreast of all pertinent laws and understand their effect on the district.

One question often asked is, "Should the chief negotiator be an attorney?" The answer is that bargaining competence is more important than general legal knowledge. Negotiating teams should always have access to legal advice, but it is not necessary for the chief negotiator to be an attorney, nor is it necessary that an attorney be on the bargaining team. One word of caution: Do not place the board attorney on the negotiating team unless he possesses expertise in collective bargaining and labor law. The selection of a novice to negotiate, no matter how well intentioned, usually results in disaster.

The IELRA and the body of law created by Labor Board decisions have powerful and far-reaching effects on any school district. The negotiator must keep abreast of Labor Board rulings that are often complex or obtuse and be able to apply those rulings to management strategy and tactics.

If the board does not have a professional negotiator, the school labor attorney should be consulted for legal advice before the bargaining team agrees to any contract language and — although it may be too late — should review any contract before the board adopts it.

A primary reason for selecting the chief negotiator prior to the selection of any other team members is to allow the negotiator some input into the selection of the other team members. Other team members should be chosen to complement the abilities of the negotiator. Team members must be able to work together toward the common goal of a good contract for the board. The other team members may be selected from central office administrators (not the superintendent, unless he is the only central office administrator), principals, supervisors, and board members. Board members should only be chosen in districts where, because of size or a lack of expertise, there are not enough qualified administrators or supervisors to compose a team or where board member feedback to the total board is necessary. As long ago as 1970 the National School Boards Association passed a resolution at its annual convention stating: "The NSBA urges that school board members do not directly participate in the technical day-to-day negotiating proceedings; rather, they should obtain skilled professionals to negotiate for the board."

Management team planning

Planning and preparation prevent mistakes and save the school board from later embarrassment. Over-preparation is rarely a problem; under-preparation is often a problem.

One way the team can prepare is to assemble data and information regarding bargaining developments outside the district. These should include such things as economic packages bargained in other districts, contract language used in other districts, legislative developments regarding school funding, and the results of IELRB decisions or court cases which might influence the local contract. However, be careful in using contract language from other districts. You may be looking at their mistakes or at issues or benefits not necessary in your situation.

Another step in planning is the analysis of union demands. Often, union demands are delivered to the board of education prior to the initial planning. This gives the management team an opportunity to analyze those demands and plan strategies as the counterproposal is being readied. Analysis includes identifying items or clauses which can be agreed to rather readily, identifying items or clauses which are unacceptable, and developing compromise language proposals where desirable.

A third step in the preparation process is to determine parameters and develop strategy. In planning sessions with the board of education, the bargaining team should obtain directions from the board relative to economic and non-economic parameters. Where possible, board directions should allow room for maneuvering and negotiating. Rigid parameters make negotiating difficult and limit the team's ability to reach agreement with the other side. At the same time, if there are issues on which the board desires little or no compromise, the team should know it. Negotiations between the board and its negotiating team sometimes turn out to be more difficult than bargaining with the union. The management team must know the total board's position on the crucial items and recognize that early ideal positions may change during the process. More than one management team has negotiated a tentative contract only to discover that it had misinterpreted the board's desires. Preliminary planning and constant feedback provide the foundation upon which the management team's credibility is built. The greater the credibility, the smoother negotiations will proceed.

8. Roles and responsibilities

Role of the school board

As boards of education become involved in collective bargaining, they encounter some special roles and responsibilities for themselves and their administrators. They also encounter a relationship with a different kind of school expert — the chief negotiator.

In general, the role of the board of education is to engage in planning activities that lead to a reasonable contract with the union. Planning includes developing goals, objectives, and parameters for the negotiator. One of the most important steps is selecting the negotiator who will speak for the bargaining team. The board should then select the remaining members of the team, in consultation with the superintendent and chief negotiator.

During the negotiating process, the board and the negotiating team should maintain close communication. Usually this is best accomplished through the superintendent or his designee, who works closely with the bargaining team in addition to regular duties as chief executive. Sometimes communication can be handled best by the chief negotiator or the entire team dealing directly with the board. The total board should not get involved in at-the-table negotiations with the union. Even more important, individual board members should resist any impulse to communicate directly with the union unless so authorized by the total board.

Initial communications between the board and its bargaining team provide the team with the goals and objectives which the board would like to pursue. The board will want to establish some parameters to guide the bargaining team. There should be some flexibility, but there should be a frank indication of which issues and dollar amounts the board feels most strongly about. As negotiations proceed, the board and its team may have to modify their initial position and discuss which items the board is willing to take to impasse proceedings and which are important enough to risk a strike or take to arbitration. At some point in the process it may be necessary for the board to update and revise its original parameters. Boards should not, however, get into the habit of intentionally withholding concessions from the bargaining team that the board planned to allow into the settlement from the beginning. Such a practice weakens the credibility of the bargaining team, and the union will forestall serious bargaining until the board reveals its real bargaining positions or the union may end run the team to bargain directly with the board. Board members must have enough confidence in their negotiating team to entrust team members with their real feelings and positions, which may often change as the process unfolds.

One of the goals of the chief negotiator and the bargaining team is to negotiate a contract which the board will ratify. If communications have been regular and open between the board and the team, there should be little doubt that the agreement will be ratified. Boards, however, are obligated to carefully review the tentative agreement prior to ratification. If any part of the agreement is not satisfactory, the board retains the right to withhold ratification. Sometimes the unsatisfactory portion can be changed to the mutual satisfaction of the board and the union without returning to the negotiating table. In some rare cases it may be necessary — although extremely dangerous — to send the bargaining team back to the table to obtain a more favorable agreement. The decision to withhold ratification and send the bargaining team back to the negotiating table should be very carefully deliberated and, if possible, avoided because the consequences are potentially damaging. Withholding ratification over a major item of the contract suggests that the board and its bargaining team have not been communicating very closely and can destroy the credibility of the management negotiating team.

The school board's role in labor relations is outlined in **Table Four.**

Role of administration

The basic role of the administration is to provide resources, information, data, and general all-around support for the school board and the bargaining team prior to and during negotiations. Central office administrators as well as building administrators may be called upon to support the process by:

1) Identifying portions of the current agreement which make contract management difficult;

2) Gathering data from school districts with similar characteristics which indicate the direction settlements are taking;

Table Four — The School Board's Role In Labor Relations

As Policy Setter
- Develop parameters based on district goals.
- Select negotiator and procedures.
- Insist on employee relations goals and objectives in bargaining, in contract management, and in human relations.
- Understand unionization.

As Individual Board Members
- Develop basic understanding of bargaining.
- Distinguish labor relations from human relations.
- Don't be co-opted or used by the union to further its goals.
- Realize that the board's public position in labor disputes must be unanimous.
- Protect the confidentiality of the board's strategy.
- Don't play mediator.

At Impasse
- Understand and expect pressures.
- Establish a unanimous position with one spokesman.
- Know the legal limitations of individual board members.
- Don't stand alone; present a united school board position and get community support.

3) Developing facts about school operations which will be affected by any agreement (salary and fringe benefit costs, etc.);

4) Serving as consultant to the management bargaining team relative to any proposals being made for the new contract;

5) Serving as a permanent or temporary member of the bargaining team; and

6) Protecting the confidentiality of the board's strategy.

When the contract goes into effect, central office administrators and building principals should be put through contract management training to learn how to deal directly with the negotiated agreement. The contract has numerous implications for management of the schools and programs. The chief negotiator should help the administration ensure that the contract is administered fairly and consistently.

Building level administrators are vitally important to the bargaining process. They alone will implement the contract on a day-to-day basis. They, therefore, must be involved in developing bargaining goals and strategies and must be trained to administer the contract. Principals should also be represented on the board's bargaining team. If not, the impact of bargaining issues on the school will not be carefully considered and the contract will be poorly administered.

It becomes even more important to obtain input from principals and provide them with feedback during the bargaining process if they choose to not be represented on the bargaining team. Principals must feel some ownership in the negotiated contract if they are to manage it effectively. Moreover, principals who are left out of the process have been known to form their own unions to protect their interests.

Role of the negotiator

One of the tenets of traditional collective bargaining is that one person should be designated to speak for the bargaining team. The person so designated should be the only one responsible for across-the-table negotiations. The designee could be any person on the bargaining team, but it is usually better to identify the chief negotiator prior to the selection of the remainder of the team.

The chief negotiator must be flexible, courteous, honest, patient, and empathetic if negotiations are to be positive rather than negative. The negotiator must possess analytical and verbal skills and, most of all, be a skilled listener. In addition, the negotiator must understand education as well as collective bargaining and labor law. Knowledge of or access to state statutes, IELRB and court decisions, and arbitration rulings and interpretations is essential.

What is the role of this chief negotiator? First, the negotiator should recommend, subject to board approval, the other team members. As leader of the team, the negotiator is expected to assign specific responsibilities to team members, solicit ideas from them, and make certain that they understand the roles assigned.

Once the bargaining team is selected and assigned, the negotiator orchestrates the management team's performance during the negotiating process. Table tactics and strategies will be directed by the negotiator with the ultimate aim of obtaining agreement on a contract within the parameters established by the board.

In addition, the negotiator should be skilled in the construction and implications of contract language, so that problems in the existing contract can be modified and future problems avoided.

Finally, the negotiator (if not a professional) should recognize when it is time to call for assistance, especially legal assistance. The negotiator is not expected to possess all of the answers for every contract proposal, but should feel free to contact appropriate resource persons when there is a question to be answered.

The decision whether to obtain the services of an outside negotiator or train someone on the staff is the first and maybe most important decision the board will make. This decision is best made by first analyzing the skills, experience, and abilities of the local staff and to determine whether the conflicts inherent in the bargaining process will diminish their effectiveness in their day-to-day jobs. If no one locally has the ability or interest or if role conflicts will be detrimental to their regular job performance, the board will find that its needs are best served by obtaining qualified assistance. The negotiated agreement is too important to be negotiated by someone ill-prepared and unfamiliar with the process.

Role of the community

The subject of "community involvement" in teacher bargaining remains a difficult issue. On the one hand, the industrial model of collective bargaining requires privacy in order to work. The parties must be able to discuss proposals freely, exchange confidences, make tradeoffs, and back down without losing face.

By the same token, school boards are expected to represent the best interests of their communities. The actual conduct of bargaining is an administrative function, but the school board is expected to establish guidelines and to approve or reject the final contract based on what is best for the school district and its constituents.

On the other hand, many parents and taxpayers feel a loss of control over the destiny of their schools. They see their school boards surrendering authority over educational and financial decisions to the unions. If student services are cut to finance higher teacher salaries and decreased workloads, then a credibility gap begins to open between the school board and the public. Citizens see costs going up and services going down. Thus, there is a growing concern among many citizens that they — as well as management and labor — should be present at the bargaining table.

Although at least one state (Florida) has gone so far as to mandate bargaining in open meetings, school district bargaining in Illinois is exempt from the Open Meetings Act and all aspects of negotiations, including school board input and feedback, can be conducted in closed meetings. Moreover, both school managers and unions tend to resist public involvement in the bargaining process. The industrial model of closed bargaining between expert negotiators represents a known quantity. Both sides can look to the experience of private sector labor relations for guidance.

Where the school board enjoys an open and positive relationship with the public and vigorously defends that relationship at the bargaining table, the results of closed bargaining are generally acceptable to the community. Where the school board fails either to recognize public sentiment or to defend the public interest, the contract settlement arrived at privately risks public disaffection. And public dissatisfaction destroys credibility.

Closed bargaining, of course, does not always remain closed. When negotiations break down and the union turns to the public to seek support, the public will become directly embroiled in the dispute.

The complexity of the labor-management relationship in education is compounded by the fact that both sides sense the importance of "good PR" when negotiations reach a stalemate. Unlike bargaining in the private sector, school bargaining is heavily influenced by the need for public approval (or the fear of negative public opinion). Teacher unions, in particular, employ a wide array of communications strategies in order to generate public support when teachers anticipate striking. How the board reads public opinion often determines the ultimate outcome of a strike and the board that misreads the sentiments of its community may agree to a contract settlement that the community does not approve of or cannot afford.

What striking teachers fail to realize, of course, is that a strike often says far more about their priorities than mere words can begin to offset.

School boards, too, frequently fail to accurately understand public attitudes and the impact that their actions have on those attitudes. Consequently, citizens are sometimes subjected to biased opinions from both sides, specialized information that is intelligible to only a few, or a running barrage of charges and counter-charges. Yet, public attitudes toward the parties are determined far more by their actions than by their words. Whether the subject is bargaining in general or a stalemate or strike, the parties demonstrate by their deeds how they feel about the public, the schools, and their labor relations. Boards are much more vulnerable to public pressure than unions because their meetings provide a forum for expression of discontent.

Labor relations surely ranks very low as a topic that people want to know about. Citizens are much more interested in student progress and in educational programs and their costs. There is much evidence, however, that the interest of parents and taxpayers comes quickly alive when schools are closed by a strike or when the school board agrees to a contract settlement that curtails parental rights or forces program cuts.

Obviously, school boards are well advised to strive for contract settlements consistent with community sentiment and to keep the community informed of their labor relations objectives.

9. Disputes

Impasse

Although the goal of the negotiations process is to reach agreement and then live by that agreement, a dispute can arise that results in an impasse. This can occur during bargaining or be produced by a grievance during the implementation of the contract.

School board members who are experienced in private sector labor relations will find another important difference with Illinois school bargaining. In the private sector, a collective bargaining impasse is the point at which the employer may implement its final offer as well as the point at which the union may strike. The definition of impasse in Illinois school bargaining is so subjective that there is no way to be certain that impasse exists until either the union strikes or the Labor Board imposes mediation. For all practical purposes, therefore, the school board is effectively precluded from unilaterally declaring impasse and imposing a settlement. Bargaining, in other words, may go on forever if no settlement is reached, if the union does not strike, or if the employer is unable to ascertain that impasse exists so a settlement can be imposed.

In 1988, the IELRB ruled that impasse exists when further negotiations would be futile and said the following factors must be examined to determine whether an impasse exists: the bargaining history and good faith of the parties; the length of negotiations; the importance of the issues unsettled; and the understanding of the parties as to the status of negotiations.

Obviously a school board that decides on its own that impasse exists does so at its own risk.

The Illinois Educational Labor Relations Act prescribes some steps for resolving an impasse during the bargaining process, although there are some options available to the parties.

Mediation

The first step prescribed by law is that of mediation. Either party may declare impasse and seek mediation 45 days before the beginning of the school year. Unless extended by mutual agreement, mediation must be requested 15 days before the beginning of the school year if a settlement has not been reached (or 15 days before the expiration of the collective bargaining agreement in the case of support staff).

Mediation involves selecting an impartial observer, usually someone with mediation experience, to assist in bringing the two sides together. If the school board and union cannot agree on a mediator, the IELRB may invoke mediation on its own motion. Most school districts call on the Federal Mediation and Conciliation Service (FMCS), which provides mediators at no charge when requested by both parties.

There are no decisions rendered by the mediator; everything is advisory. The mediator does not make judgments. The mediator's role is to persuade the parties to modify their positions and to provide ideas and suggestions to bring the issues to closure. Sometimes the mediator is successful in getting one or both sides to move closer to an agreement, but not quite enough for an actual agreement. Other times the respective positions are so rigid that there is virtually no movement by either side. If the two parties reach agreement during mediation, the impasse is resolved. If an agreement is not reached, then the impasse resolution process usually moves to the next step.

Fact-finding

Fact-finding can be the next step, if jointly requested by the parties, although many negotiators on both sides of the table are not enthused with any neutral step beyond mediation. Because the IELRA does not authorize fact-finding, it rarely occurs except in contracts pre-dating the 1983 statute.

The fact-finding process involves selecting a mutually satisfactory fact-finder, either a neutral individual or a three-member panel (one from each party plus a neutral chairperson). The fact-finder conducts an investigation of the situation in an effort to identify all of the issues still unresolved. Depending upon the language of the bargaining agreement, the fact-finder will either point out potential settlement possibilities or make a precise recommendation for resolution of the impasse. If both parties accept the fact-finder's recommendation, the dispute is resolved. Neither party, however, is bound to accept fact-finding recommendations. The fact-finding step is purely advisory. However, refusal of the fact-finder's award usually results in poor public relations and a weakened position.

Fact-finding and advisory arbitration are essentially the same in that advisory arbitration means that the two parties are not bound to accept the arbitrator's decision.

Arbitration

If mediation and fact-finding do not produce an end to the impasse, the next possible step is arbitration. There are several types of arbitration which operate in both the private and public sectors and none are popular with boards of education, because arbitration sometimes allows a neutral third party to make decisions which rightfully belong to the board.

1) Interest arbitration refers to arbitration used to resolve impasse during contract negotiations. Interest arbitration is voluntary when both parties have to agree to submit disputed issues to arbitration and is compulsory if required by law or by contract. Binding arbitration means that the two parties are bound to follow the decision of the arbitrator, while advisory arbitration is similar to fact-finding. The IELRA permits binding interest arbitration as an alternative to strikes by school employees but does not require it.

2) Grievance arbitration refers to the use of an arbitrator to interpret the meaning of the contract when a grievance is filed, claiming a violation of the contract by the employer. Illinois law requires a grievance procedure ending in binding arbitration.

While grievance arbitration is required in school board contracts, interest arbitration is not compulsory and is rarely used except as a political tactic during a work stoppage. Although it is attractive to parents when schools are closed and no settlement appears imminent, school boards almost never agree to binding interest arbitration and vigorously oppose efforts to legislate it. Binding arbitration shifts decision making authority away from the school board to a third party and is, therefore, viewed as a serious encroachment upon school board authority.

Grievances and grievance procedures

Disputes between employees and management which arise from the implementation or interpretation of the negotiated contract are referred to as "grievances." Of course, an employee might have a complaint about almost anything connected with the operation of the schools. However, formal grievances and grievance procedures should be limited to disputes directly related to the implementation or interpretation of the agreement. Language to limit the definition of a grievance to violations of the collective bargaining agreement should be included in the negotiated contract so that grievances cannot be extended to board policies, rules, and regulations.

The grievance procedure is a tool the union uses to enforce the contract. As with most tools, the grievance procedure is used and abused. School employee unions have been known to politicize the tool to harass particular administrators. They also try to broaden the scope of the contract by grieving things not already in the contract, unless proper contract language can restrict this tactic. Some grievances are simply political, either the strategic need of the union to express itself or appease a particular member(s).

Basically, the grievance procedure provides an orderly

process for the handling of grievances brought by an employee against the contract administrator. The grievance procedure should include the definition of a grievance and specific steps to be followed to achieve a resolution of the dispute. Each step should be accompanied by specific time limits which keep the process moving while allowing the administrator at that particular step enough time to make a decision. The procedure should also include specific provisions for appeal and identify and provide parameters for invoking the final step — which is binding arbitration under the IELRA.

The availability of binding arbitration makes it unwise to provide a preliminary appeal to the school board where the union can first seek a possible political response as an alternative to the final step. The astute contract manager will solicit legal and board input early in the process. Resolution of grievances should occur as early as possible.

Right to strike

The IELRA sanctions the right of educational employees to withhold services by authorizing a procedural or "limited right to strike." In Illinois, a school strike is not permitted by law except where:

- employees are represented by an exclusive bargaining agent;
- mediation has been used without success;
- at least five days have elapsed after the union has given a notice of intent to strike;
- the bargaining agreement has expired;
- unresolved issues have not been submitted to arbitration.

One effect of the Illinois law is to prohibit strikes by school employees during the term of their negotiated contract.

Some states enact laws that constrain, limit or simply prohibit strikes by school employees. Such well-meaning laws ignore a clear lesson from the private sector — that collective bargaining is a power relationship — and try to place school bargaining in an idealized setting in which employer and employee engage in rational discussion and neither party ever resorts to force. The result is that the public employee unions break the law (by striking anyway) or settle for a kind of pseudo-bargaining known as "meeting and conferring" or have final agreements determined by a neutral (arbitrator).

Teacher union leaders in Illinois and elsewhere have made it clear that they will not settle for "meet and confer" and have stood ready and willing to accept the martyrdom of jail sentences and heavy fines that have been imposed on public sector strikers. Stated simply, those who advocate public sector bargaining combined with a ban on strikes overlook the power nature of negotiations and the role that the strike threat plays in establishing a balance of that power.

However, the traditional argument against allowing strikes in public employment remains overwhelmingly strong and has yet to be adequately rebutted. That argument says that most governmental operations are established by the public as monopolies to provide services for which there are no readily available substitutes. The powerful role which competition plays in the private sector rarely exists to discipline or modify the goals of the parties in the public sector. Public sector contract settlements, therefore, often come at the expense of the public, with little regard for budgetary or market realities. So the argument remains: If the strike right is granted in public employment, there is a large risk that strong organizations will benefit at the expense of the unorganized, of relatively small and unimportant organizations, and of the public at-large.

In sum, if collective bargaining does not work well without the strike, and if the strike makes little or no sense in the public sector, large doubts remain as to the wisdom in the long run of attempting to provide, by statute, negotiating rights to public employees. Those doubts have not, however, prevented the proliferation of collective bargaining laws throughout the country. The political clout of public sector unions is too strong for legislatures to ignore.

10. When teachers strike

What can school board members expect if their teachers or other employees strike? The answer depends a great deal on whether the district has experienced strikes in the past. Members of a board that is struck for the first time may likely find the experience a little like a nasty political campaign marked by painful mud-slinging where nobody wins. Subsequent strikes tend to be a little less acrimonious.

Workers go on strike to pressure the school board into accepting the union's proposals. They expect the board to be pressured by the community (primarily parents and students) and by the prospect of students being denied essential educational opportunities.

Union leaders may have another reason for supporting a strike — the need to strengthen employee support for the union by engaging in an emotional, unifying activity. The stronger the union in terms of member loyalty, the less likely it will treat a strike as a morale-building ploy and the less likelihood of a truly nasty strike.

In any event, the union will strive to create community pressure on the board to force a favorable strike settlement.

Strike preparations

A strike presents the management team with a number of duties. For example, protecting the schools from vandalism should be part of the "strike management" plan of every school board and administration. Security very likely will involve only non-union employees working with law enforcement officials.

But a strike changes a lot of things that certain people must know about. Parents, non-striking employees, vendors and other affected third parties need to know what to do. Is the district open for business? What should students do?

Steps for communicating with the public and dealing with union negotiations should be parts of the same strategy and should be worked out among the board, administration and professional negotiations consultants. Because there can be no delay in getting word to parents and others about the status of their schools, the board team needs to have its strategy in place long before the union announces its strike.

Because state law requires at least a five-day notice, some advance warning is required. Unfortunately, the strike can occur any time after five days and, therefore, may occur with virtually no practical notice at all.

The struck school board is faced with a diverse array of options ranging from efforts to open schools in spite of the strike to a total lockout of all union employees. The school board also must decide how it will deal with the union and what to tell the public.

School boards who are served with an intent to strike notice should immediately formulate a "strike plan." This plan should be completed and ready for implementation at any time. A good strike plan addresses the following matters:

- Feasibility of an injunction.
- Whether schools should be open or closed.
- Responsibility for coordinating the overall plan.
- Plans for the principals.
- Plans for clerical and non-certified staff.
- Plans for students.
- Plans for building security.
- Plans for substitutes and working employees.
- Communication plans and public relations.
- Transportation plans.
- Continuation of negotiations.
- Continuation or termination of employee benefits.
- Status of extra-curricular activities.
- Return-to-work policy.
- List of key community officials.

Appropriate planning which anticipates as many of the above concerns as possible will avoid confusion. Board prepar-

edness can demoralize strikers. Unpreparedness can be a ca-
tastrophe.

Even where these functions are handled according to plan,
however, individual board members often confront problems
for which there is little or no help available. They will have to
deal with pressures placed on them by teachers and well-
meaning parents.

Negotiations strategy

When it first becomes apparent that the teachers are likely to strike, the school board needs to examine its position on
the issues. Far too many boards wait until the strike is un-
derway and the heat from parents and teachers has become
unbearable before deciding to sweeten their offer. They take a
hard line on salaries, for example, and then cave in after the
pressure mounts. Boards should remember this principle:

*Unless a union feels it needs a strike to build its own
strength, it is easier to get a settlement before a strike than during a strike.*

If the board is going to give the teachers another one percent increase on the salary schedule, consider how much better it is to give it before the teachers strike. Backing down
after a strike is in progress has the benefit of getting a settlement that reopens schools and reduces morale problems, of
course. But the appearance of "caving in" also casts a dark
shadow on the board's credibility and sets a precedent that
encourages future strikes.

Giving the union that additional one percent increase
before a strike may not prevent a strike, of course. In fact, if
the teachers proceed to strike anyway, the board may feel it
should have held back the one percent until teachers were
ready to settle. (One approach is to offer the additional one
percent privately or informally so that, even if refused, it can
be used later to help the union save face.) But the school board
that sticks to its guns will retain its credibility and discourage
future strikes. Not "caving in" may lead to a long and acrimonious strike that weakens the union, but the board most like-

ly will have demonstrated fiscal responsibility and created an opportunity for compromise.

Probably the most difficult task facing a chief administrator or professional negotiations consultant is to get members of a school board to agree on a position on the issues and then stick to it when the pressure mounts. The union strategy is to divide and conquer, picking off one board member at a time, until a board majority is ready to give in to bargaining demands. (Some union strategists say, "Pick 'em out and wear 'em out.")

Just as they should avoid weakening under pressure, board members must resist the temptation to strike back or get even. Avoid the temptation to take the strike personally or to make heated decisions. Neither the board nor its individual members should make intemperate or premature statements about the unreasonableness of teachers or threaten to open schools in spite of the strike or to dock teacher salaries for lost days. Any concessions that must be made at the end of the strike won't square with the earlier tough talk, and the board's public credibility will pay a big price.

Perhaps the best advice for board members and administrators alike during a strike: *Keep your eye on your real goal and remember that the strike will eventually end, but schools must keep going.* Seek to make the long-term impact of the strike as favorable as possible.

Dealing with lost school days

A school strike usually creates another bargaining issue that becomes as important as the issues that caused the strike — makeup days vs. dock days. Because most school employees work less than a full school year, it is possible to extend the school calendar into the summer so that the strike does not result in a loss of annual income for striking employees. The automatic loss of wages that befalls private sector strikers can be overcome in the school setting by bargaining back lost days.

The issue of docking or not docking becomes a real dilemma for the school board. On the one hand, the absence of economic penalties will encourage future strikes. On the other hand, if instructional time is not made up, the school board will be viewed as shortchanging its students. And you can be assured that the union will demand — at least initially — the makeup of all strike days as a condition for settling the strike.

Probably the best labor relations answer is to balance the bargaining realities with all the political and practical concerns, consider all the variables, seek compromise the same as with other bargaining issues, and insist on some degree of economic penalty for striking employees. Effective arguments in favor of docking at least some lost days is that extending school into the summer is inconvenient for families and provides only limited educational value.

The financial impact of lost school days can support either docking days or makeup days, depending upon the proportion of the school budget that comes from state aid. A school district's general state aid is reduced by 1/176th for each day less than the 176-day minimum term that schools are open. A school district that derives little income from general state aid can actually save money by docking strike days because its daily state aid loss is less than its reduced expenses. A district that relies heavily on state aid, however, may see a net loss when strike days are not made up.

Because some days will probably be made up eventually, it is usually recommended that non-striking groups or individuals be sent home and be ready to report if called. Exceptions are 12-month employees and those needed to maintain the buildings. If cooks, bus drivers and other partial-year employees with no work to do report to work, then when and if strike days are made up they will have to be paid for the additional days. Boards usually guarantee the regular work year for these employees and keep them away from the buildings and the dilemma of crossing a picket line.

Breaking a strike

There are two lawful ways to open schools in the face of a strike, neither of which holds much hope of working for an

Illinois school board.

The first way is the court injunction. A judge may order strikers back to work if the school board can show that the strike endangers the health and safety of the community. Illinois courts, however, have been reluctant to rule that the loss of school time is a health and safety issue. Moreover, any legal action during a strike is risky because judges are elected officials who will be inclined to intervene politically instead of judicially. Any political intervention — by judges, governors, legislators or mayors — will turn the balance of power to the union. Teachers have far more votes and campaign funds than school board members.

If the strike drags on and pressure builds to get schools reopened, then the school board may consider the second option — hiring substitutes and trying to operate schools during the strike. Although this option appears to be an ideal employer response, it is difficult if not impossible in Illinois because:

1) The State Board of Education requires 50 percent attendance at each grade level every day to qualify for state aid. Many parents will keep their children at home out of union allegiance or sympathy, or fear of angering their children's teachers.

2) The State Board also requires that every teacher in every class be certified to teach that class or subject. Except in very small districts, there are not enough qualified substitutes available both in total and in specific subject areas.

3) Unions will apply tremendous pressure on substitutes who "scab" and cross picket lines. This adds to the difficulty of properly staffing every classroom.

4) Picket line confrontations create emotional issues that increase union solidarity behind the strike and community sympathy for the union's cause.

5) An injunction or restraining order may become necessary to maintain order, bringing into the political mix a judge who may try to mediate or even arbitrate.

6) Non-striking employee unions will be brought into the negotiations and may even refuse to work, creating another

legal/labor battle.

The possibility of opening schools is a useful "hammer" in the school board's box of strike tools. In fact, some school boards have successfully opened a few schools in lengthy strikes simply to provide child care for the community — and remove some parental pressures. However, the political and practical problems that come with efforts to open schools with a State Board-approved program make it advisable only in extreme situations.

Resisting pressure tactics

When teachers strike, members of the school board, the superintendent, and a few members of the top management team will find themselves encircled and isolated. Teacher union tactics almost always produce an initial surge of parent and student support, which in turn fuels the teachers' emotional fires. The board and administration will become the objects of considerable spite, particularly at the outset of a first strike. People who formerly sought out your company will be nowhere in sight. Board members whose livelihoods depend upon the goodwill of teachers and parents will feel especially vulnerable. It will be a terribly lonely feeling.

The longer a strike lasts, the more anxious rank-and-file strikers become about their jobs and paychecks and the more emotion a union must generate in order to keep up morale. That often means more harassment of individual board members and more negative publicity disseminated by the union.

Instances of truly vicious strike tactics have become relatively rare in recent years. In the early years of school union organizing, it was not uncommon for school board members to experience vandalism, boycotts of their private businesses, picketing at their homes and threats of much worse. The negative effect of such tactics on public sentiment toward teachers and their unions proved counterproductive, of course, so they tend to occur today only when anger gets completely out of control.

However, more subtle union tactics also can be effective

when they harass or pressure board members. The union, for example, may publish the names and telephone numbers of school board members, who then receive numerous phone calls from people they don't know. Acquaintances and community leaders also can be called upon to pressure board members, who are generally made to feel alone against the world.

If it happens, be of good courage. You are not alone. The same thing has happened to every school board that has ever gone through a strike. Moreover, the tide will go out just as surely as the tide came in. If the board and administration can resist the temptation to retaliate, public opinion should reverse itself and turn on the union.

Unions win the settlements they want when (a) the board is stampeded into quick concession before public opinion shifts or (b) the board attacks the teachers in public, thereby lending credence to all the nasty things the teachers had been saying.

School boards win reasonable strike settlements when (a) they remain calm, courageous and reasonable in the face of strident union attacks and (b) seek to negotiate a settlement at the table rather than in public forums.

If board members need help keeping up their courage, arrangements should be made for them to speak confidentially with other board members who have experienced a strike or with the staff or leaders of their state school boards association.

11. Concluding recommendations

To adjust management style to deal with the problems and constraints of collective bargaining, school boards and superintendents should consider the following recommendations:

1) Recognize the legal status of collective bargaining in Illinois schools. The IELRA, which grants school employee unions the right to represent their members in collective bargaining with school boards, was enacted at the urging of the teachers unions and establishes the rules by which school boards must play the bargaining game.

2) Recognize the realities of adversary collective bargaining — the intervention of the union between employee and employer and the implied threat to administrative authority and to staff involvement procedures. Also recognize that few school boards have the necessary experience and skills and few are prepared politically, psychologically or emotionally to deal with the process without preparation and assistance.

3) Understand the historical and psychological pressures that have resulted in formalized unions; the needs and the pressures of the faculty; the competition among the unions for recognition status; the conflicts between the union and non-union sympathizers during the organizational phase; and the initial response of inexperienced administrators to avoid or circumvent the process or make concessions to delay unionization.

4) Recognize the constraints peculiar to school bargaining: an elusive and distant source of revenue controlled by the legislature; traditions of teacher input or shared authority in governance which will be threatened by both union and management; extreme pressures from state-level union leaders whose goals are often unrelated to the diverse needs of teachers at the district level; faculty individuality which will collide with egalitarian union concepts; and traditions of informal evaluation and classroom freedom which must meet the test of adversary bargaining.

5) Recognize that the key issues will be benefits, working conditions, security and grievance procedures. Do not get emotionally involved in fighting windmills, such as recognition itself, affiliation, union propaganda, representation, procedures, and personalities.

6) Accept the pressures of adversary bargaining. Attempts to circumvent reality or to develop informal collegial models may result in frustration and impasse unless carefully planned and orchestrated by skilled negotiators. Select as negotiators individuals who understand the system, the constraints, and the realities of bargaining at the public school level and whose major aim is to reach an agreement acceptable to both parties, not to either "bust" the union (by management) or create explosive issues to develop solidarity (by the union).

7) Recognize that collective bargaining does not automatically bring forth unlimited benefits, nor does it automatically destroy the existing structure of governance or administration. Successful bargaining from the union standpoint depends upon realistic expectations of the membership so that the union can bring systematic and regular gains to its clients. Successful bargaining for management requires establishing reasonable strategies and goals to protect its important interests while allowing for union gains. Successful bargaining will, therefore, be conciliatory rather than traumatic, tense but not explosive.

8) Recognize that collective bargaining does formalize policies and procedures; that it results in a rigid legal document; that it equalizes and levels rather than allowing for individual differences; that it is pedantic, not pedagogic; that unions will tend to form bureaucracies very similar to managements; and that it requires a basic understanding by all involved, not just by the chief negotiator, if it is to be nonthreatening.

9) Distinguish between labor relations and human relations. Have programs in both, but keep them separate and distinct, recognizing their differences as well as their values. Both union and management must be aware that the most satisfied employee is one who feels positive toward management *and* the union. Destroying the other side also destroys the working relationship and increases tension. To achieve this equilibrium requires a great deal of effort in negotiating and managing a contract, and in understanding the needs, views, and pressures of the other party.

10) Understand the political pressures, particularly at impasse, and the importance of confidentiality, consensus, and unanimity of positions and support from the entire school board and administrative team.

11) Recognize that the most important objective is an end product (contract) that is not restrictive — that is, one that does not prevent the organization from providing the best educational program possible. Don't let frustrations with the process lead to an alternative process that sacrifices control of the outcomes.

12) Understand the law and the limits that it places on establishing policy, particularly on mandatory subjects of bargaining which require decisional bargaining prior to taking action.

13) Understand that policies and past practices related to employee working conditions cannot be changed without notice and bargaining (after a bargaining unit has been created).

14) Understand the importance of good faith bargaining and IELRB decisions in defining and describing the obligation to bargain terms and conditions of employment.

Appendix A — Some Important Provisions of the Illinois Educational Labor Relations Act

The Illinois Educational Labor Relations Act (IELRA) is found in the state statutes at 115 ILCS 5/1 et seq. Note that references to "Board" in material quoted from the Act refer to the Illinois Educational Labor Relations Board. The local school board is referred to as the "educational employer."

EMPLOYER COVERAGE

The scope of employer coverage under the Illinois Educational Labor Relations Act is confined strictly to public sector educational employers. The definition of "educational employer" includes public school districts, combinations of public school districts, joint agreements formed by two or more school districts, public community colleges, state colleges or universities, and any State agency whose major function is providing educational services.

EMPLOYEE COVERAGE

IELRA defines "educational employee" as any full- or part-time employee of an educational employer except elected officials, gubernatorial appointees, firefighters, supervisors, managerial employees, confidential employees, short-term employees, students, and part-time academic employees of community colleges.

"Supervisor" is "any individual having authority in the interests of the employer to hire, transfer, suspend, lay off, recall, promote, discharge, reward or discipline other employees within the appropriate bargaining unit and adjust their grievances; or to effectively recommend such action if the exercise of such authority is not of a merely routine or clerical nature but requires the use of independent judgment. The term 'supervisor' includes only those individuals who devote a preponderance of their employment time to such exercising of authority."

"Managerial Employee" is "an individual who is engaged predominantly in executive and management functions and is charged with the effectuation of such management policies and practices."

"Confidential Employee" is "an employee, who (i) in the regular course of his/her duties, assists and acts in a confidential capacity to persons who formulate, determine and effectuate management policies with regard to labor relations or who (ii) in the regular course of his/her duties has access to information relating to the effectuation or review of the employer's collective bargaining policies."

The definition of "professional employee," for the purposes of public school districts, encompasses any certificated employee.

A "craft employee" is a "skilled journeyman, crafts persons, and their apprentices and helpers."

EMPLOYEE RIGHTS

Educational employees have the right "to organize, form, join, or assist in employee organizations or engage in lawful concerted activities for the purpose of collective bargaining or other mutual aid and protection or bargain collectively through representatives of their own free choice." Except as provided for in a fair share clause contained in a collective bargaining agreement, educational employees "also have the right to refrain from any or all such activities."

Even though an employee may be represented by an exclusive bargaining representative, "any individual employee or group of employees may at any time present grievances to their employer and have them adjusted without the intervention of the bargaining representative as long as the adjustment is not inconsistent with the terms of a collective bargaining agreement then in effect, provided that the bargaining representative has been given an opportunity to be present at such adjustment."

EMPLOYER RIGHTS

Employers have the right to refrain from bargaining "over matters of inherent managerial policy," described below under "Duty to Bargain/Scope of Bargaining."

UNIT DETERMINATION STANDARDS

It is the responsibility of the Educational Labor Relations Board to determine an appropriate bargaining unit. The factors for determining an appropriate bargaining unit are the "historical pattern of recognition, community of interest, including employee skills and functions, degree of functional integration, interchangeability and contact among employees, common supervision, wages, hours and other working conditions of the employees involved, and the desires of the employees." Professional and nonprofessional employees may not be in the same bargaining unit unless a majority in each group vote for inclusion in such unit. Also, "where the majority of public employees of a craft so decide, the Board shall designate such craft as a unit appropriate for the purposes of collective bargaining." Finally, "multi-unit bargaining" is not prohibited.

DUTY TO BARGAIN/SCOPE OF BARGAINING

IELRA provides that "a public employer and the exclusive representative have the authority and duty to bargain" and defines "collective bargaining" as "the performance of the mutual obligations of the educational employer and the representative of the educational employees to meet at reasonable times and confer in good faith with respect to wages, hours and other terms and conditions of employment." The obligation to bargain collectively, however, "does not compel either party to agree to a proposal or require the making of a concession."

Once an agreement is reached and ratified by the parties, IELRA requires the parties to reduce such agreement to writing.

The collective bargaining agreement negotiated by the parties must contain a grievance procedure that terminates in binding arbitration. The collective bargaining agreement must "also contain appropriate language prohibiting strikes for the duration of the agreement."

IELRA limits the scope of bargaining ("wages, hours, and other terms and conditions of employment") by not requiring employers "to bargain over matters of inherent managerial policy, which shall include such areas of discretion or policy as the functions of the employer, standards of services, its overall budget, the organizational structure and selection of new employees and direction of employees." However, employers "shall be required to bargain collectively with regard to policy matters directly affecting wages, hours, and terms and conditions of employment as well as the impact thereon upon request by employee representatives."

The Act prohibits provisions in a collective bargaining agreement that would violate or conflict with existing statutes. Provisions, however, are permitted which implement or supplement, but not diminish or negate, any existing statutory rights and benefits pertaining to wages, hours and other terms and conditions of employment.

UNION SECURITY

A collective bargaining agreement may include a provision requiring non-union members to pay a fair share fee to the union for services rendered. The amount certified by the exclusive representative to the employer shall not exceed "the dues uniformly required of members." In addition, the "amount certified by the exclusive representative shall not include any fees for contributions related to the election or support of any candidate for political office." Nothing, however, precludes voluntary political contributions by the nonmember. Finally, fair share agreements must also protect the rights of nonmembers whose non-affiliation is based upon "bonafide religious tenets." Such nonmembers shall contribute an amount equal to the fair share payment to a nonreligious charitable organization.

UNFAIR LABOR PRACTICES

Under IELRA, educational employers are prohibited from:

"1) Interfering, restraining or coercing employees in the exercise of the rights guaranteed under this Act.

"2) Dominating or interfering with the formation, existence or administration of any employee organization.

"3) Discriminating in regard to hire or tenure of employment or any term or condition of employment to encourage or discourage membership in any employee organization.

"4) Discharging or otherwise discriminating against an employee because he or she has signed or filed an affidavit, authorization card, petition or complaint or given any information or testimony under this Act.

"5) Refusing to bargain collectively in good faith with an employee representative which is the exclusive representative of employees in an appropriate unit, including but not limited to the discussing of grievances with the exclusive representative; provided, however, that if an alleged unfair labor practice involves interpretation or application of the terms of a collective bargaining agreement and said agreement contains a grievance and arbitration procedure, the Board may defer the resolution of such dispute to the grievance and arbitration procedure contained in said agreement.

"6) Refusing to reduce a collective bargaining agreement to writing and signing such agreement.

"7) Violating any of the rules and regulations promulgated by the Board regulating the conduct of representation elections.

"8) Refusing to comply with the provisions of a binding arbitration award."

Additionally, employee organizations are prohibited from:

"1) Restraining or coercing employees in the exercise of

the rights guaranteed under this Act.

"2) Restraining or coercing an educational employer in the selection of his representative for the purpose of collective bargaining or the adjustment of grievances.

"3) Refusing to bargain collectively in good faith with an educational employer, if they have been designated in accordance with any provisions of this Act as the exclusive representative of employees in an appropriate unit.

"4) Violating any of the rules and regulations promulgated by the Board regulating the conduct of representation elections.

"5) Refusing to reduce a collective bargaining agreement to writing and signing such agreement.

"6) Refusing to comply with the provisions of a binding arbitration award."

UNFAIR LABOR PRACTICE PROCEDURES

Unfair labor practice charges are filed with the Labor Board. If an investigation by the Board reveals that the charge states an issue of law or fact, then the Board shall issue a complaint stating the charges and conduct a hearing. Also, if "the Board finds that the party charged has committed an unfair labor practice, it shall make findings of fact and is empowered to issue an order requiring the party charged to stop the unfair labor practice." In addition, the Labor Board "may take additional affirmative action, including requiring the party to make reports from time to time showing the extent to which he or she has complied with the order." All unfair labor practice charges must be filed within six months of the event giving rise to the charge.

IMPASSE PROCEDURES

IELRA contains the following impasse procedures:

1) In the case of an existing exclusive bargaining representative, bargaining must begin within 60 days of receipt by a party of a demand to bargain. In the case of a newly certified exclusive bargaining representative, collective bargaining

must begin within 60 days of the date of certification. Once collective bargaining has commenced, it must continue for at least 60 days unless an agreement is reached by both parties.

2) If no collective bargaining agreement has been entered into 90 days before the start of the next school year, then the parties must notify the Labor Board of the status of negotiations.

3) If no collective bargaining agreement has been entered into 45 days before the start of the next school year, either party may petition the Labor Board to initiate mediation. In addition, "the Board on its own motion may initiate mediation during this period."

4) If no collective bargaining agreement has been entered into 15 days before the start of the next school year, the Labor Board shall invoke mediation.

The impasse procedures of factfinding and arbitration used to resolve disputes over terms to be included in an existing or new collective bargaining agreement may only be engaged upon mutual agreement of the parties; i.e., factfinding and interest arbitration are permissive. Finally, the "costs of factfinding and mediation shall be shared equally between the employer and the exclusive bargaining agent."

STRIKES

IELRA grants employees the right to strike if the following conditions are met:

1) the employees are represented by an exclusive bargaining representative;

2) mediation has been unsuccessful;

3) the exclusive representative has provided the employer, regional superintendent, and Labor Board with five days notice of the intent to strike;

4) the collective bargaining agreement has expired; and

5) "the employer and the exclusive bargaining representative have not mutually submitted the unresolved issues to arbitration."

An employer may seek injunctive relief if the strike becomes a clear and present danger to the health or safety of the public." However, an "unfair labor practice or other evidence of lack of clean hands by the educational employer is a defense" to an action for injunctive relief. In addition, IELRA limits the jurisdiction of the court by incorporating the Anti-Injunction Act.

Appendix B — Glossary

Agency Shop (Fair Share) — A provision in a collective agreement which requires that all employees in the negotiating unit who do not join the exclusive representative (union) pay a fixed fee as a condition of employment, usually the equivalent of labor organization's dues excluding political action fees. An agency shop is permissible under Illinois law. *See Union Shop. See pages 16, 86.*

Agreement — A written agreement between an employer (or an association of employers) and a labor organization (or organizations), usually for a definite term, defining conditions of employment, rights of employees and the labor organization, and procedures to be followed in settling disputes or handling issues that arise during the life of the agreement. *See Collective Negotiations. See Contract.*

American Arbitration Association (AAA) — A private nonprofit organization established to aid professional arbitrators in their work through legal and technical services, and to promote arbitration as a method of settling commercial and labor disputes. The AAA provides lists of qualified arbitrators to labor organizations and employers on request.

Arbitration — Method of settling employment disputes through recourse to an impartial third party, whose decision may be final and binding. *See page 68.*

Arbitration — Advisory (Fact-Finding) — A method of settling disputes where the arbitrator's decision may be refused by either party. The arbitrator has no power to enforce a decision and can only recommend solutions. Used for both interest and grievance arbitration. *See page 67.*

Arbitration — Binding — The arbitrator's decision is final and must be accepted by both parties. A dissatisfied party can only appeal the arbitrator's ruling through the courts.

Arbitration — Compulsory — Arbitration process which is required by law or contract; the parties must submit disputes to an arbitrator. If one party calls for arbitration the other party cannot refuse to arbitrate. Grievance arbitration is compulsory under the IELRA while interest arbitration is not. Interest arbitration may be made compulsory by contractual agreement between the school board and union.

Arbitration — Grievance — A final step in a grievance procedure used to determine whether a violation, misapplication, or misinterpretation of an existing agreement has occurred. Under IELRA, the union contract must include a grievance procedure with binding arbitration. *See page 68.*

Arbitration — Interest — A process that is used to force parties to reach settlement when at impasse over terms and conditions that are to be included in an agreement. Interest arbitration may be binding or advisory (fact-finding) but is purely voluntary under IELRA. *See page 68.*

Arbitration — Voluntary — Arbitration process which is not compulsory, but which allows either party to refuse to enter into arbitration if it does not feel that the arbitrator can resolve the dispute.

Arbitrator — An impartial third party to whom disputing parties submit their differences for decision (award). An ad hoc arbitrator is one selected to act in a specific case or a limited group of cases. A permanent arbitrator is one selected to serve for the life of the agreement or a stipulated term, hearing all disputes that arise during this period.

Bargaining Agent — Organization recognized by the employer as the exclusive representative of all employees in the negotiating unit for purposes of collective negotiations.

Also: bargaining representative; labor organization; union. *See pages 6, 53, 85.*

Bargaining Unit — Group of employees recognized by the employer or group of employers, or designated by the IELRB as appropriate for representation by a labor organization for purposes of collective negotiations. *See pages 6, 53, 85.*

Boilerplate — Basic contract language necessary to regulate and implement the substantive provisions of the agreement.

Caucus — When one party or the other calls "time out" during negotiations in order to discuss strategy and/or the issues under consideration without the other party present.

Certification — Recognition of the labor organization based on the mandatory procedure for determining the exclusive representative of an appropriate unit. *See pages 6, 85.*

Collective Negotiations (Professional Negotiations) — A process whereby employees as a group and their employers make offers and counter-offers for the purpose of reaching a mutually acceptable agreement and the execution of a written document incorporating any such agreement. This term implies good faith on the part of both sides but does not require either side to make concessions to the other. *See Good Faith. See page 38.*

Confidential employee — A school district employee who, in the regular course of his duties, assists and acts in a confidential capacity to persons who formulate, determine, and effectuate management policies with regard to labor relations or has access to information relating to the effectuation or review of the employer's collective bargaining policies. A confidential employee is not covered by the IELRA. *See page 84.*

Consultation — An obligation on the part of an employer to consult with the employee organization on particular issues before taking action on them.

Contract — A written agreement that is legally enforceable. *See Agreement. See pages 33, 42, 47.*

Crisis Bargaining — Collective bargaining which takes place under the threat of an imminent strike deadline. Distinguished from "extended negotiations," in which both parties have ample time to present and discuss their positions.

Decertification — Withdrawal of a labor organization's official recognition as exclusive negotiating representative. *See Certification. See page 10.*

Decisional Bargaining — Bargaining with the union before making a management decision or implementing a change in some mandatory subject of bargaining. Distinguish from "impact bargaining." *See pages 13, 36.*

Dispute — Any disagreement between an employer and a labor organization which requires resolution in one way or another; e.g., inability to agree on contract terms or to settle a grievance.

Dues Check-off — An agreement by the employer to deduct the organization dues from the wages of union members and transmit them to the union. Dues check-off is required by Illinois law when requested by an employee.

Exclusive Negotiating Rights — The right and obligation of an employee organization designated as majority representative to negotiate for all employees in the bargaining unit, including nonmembers.

Expedited Bargaining — Contract bargaining within a condensed time frame. *See page 43.*

Fact-finding Board — A group of individuals appointed to investigate, assemble, and report the facts in an employment dispute, sometimes with authority to make recommendations for settlement. *See Advisory Arbitration. See page 67.*

Fair Share — *See Agency Shop.*

Federal Mediation and Conciliation Service (FMCS) — An independent federal agency which provides mediators to assist parties involved in negotiations or in a labor dispute; provides lists of suitable arbitrators on request; and engages in various types of "preventive mediation." Mediation services are also provided by several state agencies. *See page 67.*

Fringe Benefits — Generally, supplements to wages or salaries received by employees at a cost to employers. The term encompasses a host of practices (paid vacation, pensions, health and life insurance plans, retirement incentives, etc.). No agreement prevails as to the list of practices that should be called "fringe benefits." Other terms often substituted for "fringe benefits" include "wage extras," "hidden payroll," "non-wage labor costs," and "supplementary wage practices." *See table on page 31.*

Good Faith Bargaining — The willingness of the parties to meet and discuss bargaining issues while making, in total, a reasonable effort to reach an agreement. Good faith does not require that either party concede, compromise, or agree to any particular proposal. *See pages 26, 29, 37.*

Grievance — A complaint by an employee that a provision of the collective agreement under which he is working is being violated. *See page 69.*

Grievance Procedure — A formal plan set forth in the collective agreement which provides for the adjustment of grievances through discussions at progressively higher levels of authority in management and the employee organization. IELRA requires a grievance procedure that concludes with binding arbitration. *See pages 34, 69.*

Illinois Educational Labor Relations Act (IELRA) — Illinois law that became effective in January 1984, establishes the right of educational employees to organize and bargain collectively. It defines unfair labor practices and provides for their resolution. The purpose of the Act is to regulate labor relations between educational employers and educational employees, including the designation of employee representatives, negotiation of wages, hours and other conditions of employment, and the resolution of disputes. *See Appendix A. See pages 5, 13, 22, 53.*

Illinois Educational Labor Relations Board (IELRB) — A five-member board created by the IELRA to administer the Act. The Board employs an executive director, hearing officers and others to aid in the administration of the Act. The Board has offices in Springfield and Chicago and a website at *www.Illinois.gov/elrb/*. *See pages 5-8, 13, 22, 29, 32, 35, 37, 66, 67.*

Impact Bargaining — Mid-term bargaining that is required by law when the school board or administration takes or wants to take action on an issue that affects employee working conditions. Contrast with "decisional bargaining." *See pages 13, 34-37.*

Impasse — When the positions of both sides do not allow further concessions and agreement has not been reached. The IELRB has held that the following factors determine whether an impasse exists: the bargaining history and good faith of the parties; the length of negotiations; the importance of the issues unsettled, and the understanding of the parties as to the status of negotiations. *See pages 36, 66.*

Injunction — A court order restraining one or more persons or unions from performing some act which the court believes would result in irreparable injury to property or other rights. May be a temporary injunction or a permanent injunction. *See pages 77, 90.*

Interest-Based Bargaining — Like Win-Win Bargaining, interest-based bargaining is an alternative approach to negotiations. Also called "integrative bargaining," interest-based bargaining seeks to focus on identifying and meeting the real needs or interests of both parties. *See page 43. Also see Win-Win Bargaining.*

Labor Management Relations Act of 1947 (Taft-Hartley Act) — Federal law, amending the National Labor

Relations Act of 1935 (Wagner Act). The Taft-Hartley Act defined and made illegal a number of unfair labor practices by unions and retained the definition of unfair practices as applied to employers. The act does not apply to employees in a business or industry where a labor dispute would not affect interstate commerce. Other major exclusions are: employees subject to the Railway Labor Act, agricultural workers, government employees, domestic servants, and supervisors. Amended by Labor Management Reporting and Disclosure Act of 1959 (Landrum-Griffin Act).

Lockout — When the employer takes action to prevent employees from coming to work, usually as a response to impasse and strike actions of employees. *See page 73.*

Maintenance of Standards (Past Practice) Clause — A contract provision which prevents employers from making any changes in existing employment practices or policy without negotiating the change with the employee organization even if such changes are not considered in the agreement. Automatically broadens the scope of negotiations to cover every conceivable personnel policy or action. *See Past Practice.*

Management Rights — The rights reserved to management which may be expressly noted as such in a collective agreement. Under the IELRA, employers have the right to refrain from bargaining "over matters of inherent managerial policy, which shall include such areas of discretion or policy as the functions of the employer, standards of service, its overall budget, the organizational structure and selection of new employees and direction of employees." *See pages 30, 35, 85.*

Managerial Employee — An employee who is engaged predominantly in executive and management functions and is charged with directing the effectuation of management policies and practices. A managerial employee is not covered by the IELRA. *See page 84.*

Mediation — Informal attempt by a third party to help in the settlement of an employment dispute through persuasion, advice or other suggestions, but without specific public recommendations for settlement. Under IELRA, mediation may be invoked by either the school board or the union or, under some circumstances, by the IELRB. *See pages 67, 89.*

Meet and Confer — Informal negotiations which do not result in collective bargaining agreements and/or recognized collective bargaining agents. *See page 12.*

Memorandum of Understanding (Side Letter) — An agreement between two parties that is not incorporated into the contract but is enforceable through the contract interpretation procedures.

Mid-term Bargaining (Interim Bargaining) — Bargaining that takes place while a collective bargaining agreement is in force. Occurs when management wishes to take an action on a matter that affects terms and conditions of employment. *See pages 34, 35.*

National Labor Relations Act of 1935 (Wagner Act) — Basic federal act guaranteeing to private-sector employees the right to organize and bargain collectively through representatives of their own choosing. The Act also defined "unfair labor practices" as regards employers. It was amended by the Labor Management Relations Act of 1947 and the Labor-Management Reporting and Disclosure Act of 1959. *See page 4.*

No-strike Clause — A provision in a collective agreement in which the employee organization agrees not to strike during the term of the agreement. The IELRA requires each school district labor contract to contain a no-strike clause. *See page 70.*

Packaging — Combining unresolved bargaining issues in order to make offers on many items rather than considering each issue separately. *See page 40.*

Past Practices — Working conditions covered by current policies and procedures, which cannot be altered except through collective bargaining or mid-term bargaining. *See Maintenance of Standards. See pages 12, 25, 46.*

Picketing — The patrolling near the place of employment by members of an employee organization to publicize their dispute. *See page 78.*

Ratification — The formal approval of a newly negotiated agreement by vote of the organization members or the school board. *See page 59.*

Recognition — Employer acceptance or employee election of an organization authorized to negotiate, usually for all of the members of a negotiating unit. The IELRA establishes recognition standards and procedures. *See pages 4, 6, 9.*

Reopening Clause — A provision in a collective agreement stating the time or the circumstances under which negotiations may be reopened prior to the expiration of the contract; commonly restricted to only certain provisions of the agreement rather than the agreement as a whole. *See Zipper Clause.*

Retrieval Bargaining — Negotiations in which the employer attempts to remove benefits or rights previously agreed to in a union contract. *See Status Quo. See page 24.*

Scope of Negotiations — Personnel policies and practices and other matters affecting working conditions which an employer and a labor organization will consider when negotiating an agreement. For Illinois school boards, the scope of negotiations is established by state statute and rulings of the IELRB. *See pages 13, 29, 85.*

Seniority — Term used to designate an employee's status relative to other employees, as in determining order of promotion, layoff, vacation, etc. **Straight seniority** — seniority acquired solely through length of service. **Qualified seniority** — other factors such as ability considered with length of service. **Departmental or unit**

seniority — seniority applicable in a particular department or agency rather than in the entire establishment. A "seniority list" ranks individual workers in order of seniority. By state statute, school employees in Illinois are granted certain seniority rights that govern the order of layoff. *See page 16.*

Separability Clause — A provision in a collective bargaining agreement which provides that should any part of the agreement be declared illegal by a court of competent jurisdiction, only that part is deleted from the agreement, allowing the remainder of the agreement to remain in effect.

Short-term Employee — An employee who is employed for less than two consecutive calendar quarters during a calendar year and who does not have reasonable assurance that he or she will be rehired by the same employer for the same service in a subsequent calendar year. A short-term employee is not covered by the IELRA. *See page 83.*

Side Bar — A negotiations tactic whereby chief negotiators or small groups can informally negotiate apart from the larger group without the pressure of making formal proposals.

Strike — A temporary stoppage of work by a group of employees to enforce a demand for changes in the conditions of employment or resolve a dispute with management. The right to strike is granted by the IELRA, provided that no contract is currently in force and other conditions are met. *See pages 17, 70, 72, 89.*

Status Quo — The terms, conditions and benefits of an expired contract continue in force until a new contract is agreed upon. *See page 26.*

Strike Vote — A vote conducted among members of an employee organization to determine whether or not a strike should be called.

Supervisor — Any individual having authority in the interests of the employer to hire, transfer, suspend, lay off, recall, promote, discharge, reward, or discipline other employees within the appropriate bargaining unit and adjust their grievances, or to effectively recommend such action if the exercise of such authority is not of a merely routine or clerical nature, but requires the use of independent judgment. The term "supervisor" includes only those individuals who devote a preponderance of their employment time to exercising such authority. *See page 83.*

Unfair Labor Practice — Actions which an employer and labor organization are to avoid in relating to each other throughout the collective bargaining process. Specific actions constituting unfair labor practices for both the school board and union are set forth in the IELRA. *See pages 7, 46, 87.*

Union Shop — Provision in a collective agreement that requires all employees to become members of the union within a specified time after hiring (typically 30 days) or after a new provision is negotiated, and to remain members of the union as a condition of continued employment. **Modified Union Shop** — variations on the union shop. Certain employees may be exempted, such as those already employed at the time the provision was negotiated. Union shop provisions are illegal in Illinois school districts.

Win-Win Bargaining — An alternative bargaining process designed to enhance communications and minimize confrontation. Requires joint ownership and acceptance of procedures. *See page 42.*

Zipper Clause — A contract provision specifically barring any attempt to reopen negotiations during the term of the agreement. *See Reopening Clause. See page 35.*

Appendix C — Avoid These Pitfalls in Your Teacher Union Contract

By George M. Kohut

When it's time to bargain a new teacher union contract, school boards and administrators typically focus on the obvious costs associated with the salary schedule. And rightly so. Small changes in multipliers can produce big increases in annual salary costs.

But contract proposals presented by teacher unions usually extend well beyond the salary schedule, and some of those proposals for fringe benefits can be just as costly as changes in the salary schedule. Moreover, some proposals that do not carry price tags may actually cost a great deal through the restrictions they place on management decision making and the policy making powers of the board.

The importance of all contract provisions is greatly increased by a couple of key factors. One factor is the grievance procedure that, by law in Illinois, must be included in all teachers union contracts.[1] This means that even innocent-sounding language is subject to the grievance procedure and binding arbitration.

---

[1] 115 ILCS 5/10(c)

George M. Kohut is assistant superintendent of Belleville Township High School District 201. He previously served as a school board negotiator for numerous Illinois districts during his association with the law firm of Miller, Tracy, Braun, Funk and Miller (1987 to 2005) and the Illinois Association of School Boards (1981 to 1987).

Kohut holds a doctorate in educational administration from Illinois State University. He is a frequent speaker on collective bargaining and presents workshops on labor relations for the Illinois Association of School Boards and the Illinois Association of School Administrators.

Status Quo

A second factor that makes every contract provision worthy of close attention is the concept of "status quo."

A common misconception among school board members and administrators is the belief that the expiration of a collective bargaining agreement terminates the provisions contained therein. If that were true, of course, school officials could then ignore the terms and conditions set forth in the expired contract.

However, labor law imposes the concept of "status quo" on collective bargaining in education. "Status quo" simply means that contract provisions do not end when a contract expires. Rather, any benefits provided to bargaining unit members continue in force until a new contract is mutually agreed to. "Status quo" requirements also pertain to the common management practices that the union and the administration consider normal during the ordinary course of business.

"Status quo" means that any regrettable language that might have been included in the contract does not expire unless it is negotiated out of a subsequent contract.

The cost of negotiating the removal of a bad contract provision is usually very high. That is, a union has no reason to agree with removal unless the management team offers trade-offs of significant value, usually meaning financial incentives.

Although a school board may be tempted to give away some innocuous sounding contract provision in lieu of a salary increase, the eternal nature of contract provisions and the high cost of removing them should make school boards and administrators extremely diligent in evaluating such proposals.

Fringe Benefits

Some fringe benefits — including employee health insurance and early retirement incentives — represent direct costs to the school district. However, some benefits also are governed by complex state and federal laws that can subject the unsuspecting school board to additional unanticipated costs, including penalties for violations of law. Such programs include:

• health insurance cafeteria plans, retirement plans and other benefits that call into play the federal tax code and Internal Revenue Service;

• early retirement plans that must comply with rules of the Teachers Retirement System;

• school board assumption of teacher contributions to the retirement system, another feature regulated by the federal tax code as well as state law.

The complex nature of such fringe benefits is beyond the scope of this article, but school boards and administrators need to take extra pains to ensure that such measures meet the requirements of law before accepting them in any union contract. School officials also need accurate projections of costs, both short and long term.

What follows below is a brief analysis of some non-economic contract proposals that are often presented as demands by teacher union negotiating teams. The proposals may sound innocent but their impact can be toxic. The school board and superintendent need to understand the potential impact of such demands before they end up as clauses in the final negotiated agreement.

These are just a few examples of harmful contract language. The list is by no means all inclusive.

Objectionable contract language typically proposed by the union is presented here in italic.

Employee Discipline

UNION PROPOSAL — *The board shall not discipline employees without just cause, and shall follow the practice of progressive discipline.*

As typically presented by the union negotiator, "discipline" is not defined. The administrator is left to wonder, "Is an involuntary transfer considered discipline? How about an unsatisfactory evaluation?"

"Just cause" is not an ambiguous concept. Thousands of arbitration decisions have created standards by which to establish degrees of justifiable discipline. One of the most important of these standards is the concept of mitigating factors that would excuse unacceptable behavior.

Generally, the criteria used by arbitrators when determining just cause are:

• Did the district give the employee forewarning of the likely disciplinary consequences of the employee's conduct?

• Was the district's rule or managerial order reasonably related to either the orderly and safe operation of the district's business or to the performance that the district might properly expect of the employee?

• Did the employer, before administering discipline to the employee, make an effort to discover whether the employee did in fact violate or disobey a rule or order of the employer?

• Was the district's investigation conducted fairly and objectively?

• Did the investigating administrator obtain substantial evidence or proof that the employee was guilty as charged?

• Has the district applied its rules, orders and penalties even-handedly without discrimination to all employees?

• Was the degree of discipline administered reasonably related to (a) the seriousness of the employee's proven offense and (b) the record of the employee in his service with the district?

Obviously, the burden of proof rests with the district. That is, the district will be required to prove that it followed the above steps when it administered discipline of virtually any type to an employee (including the discipline of coaches and supervisors of co-curricular programs).

The "just cause" clause in a union contract means that any action of the administrator that is perceived as discipline by the union or employee will be subjected to the above standards, including suspensions without pay and oral or written reprimands.

UNION PROPOSAL — *Prior to discharge, the following actions will be taken if an employee does not perform his or her work properly, fails to follow instructions from his or her immediate supervisor, or violates rules and regulations of school policy:*

First Notice: If an employee is not performing his or her work properly or has violated the rules and/or regulations, an oral warning will be given the employee stating the reasons his or her work has not been performed properly or that he or she has violated rules and/or regulations.

Second Notice: If a second notice is needed, the employee may receive a written warning stating the reasons that his or her work has not been performed properly or that he or she has violated work rules and/or regulations or the employee may be suspended with or without pay or discharged from his or her job with the school district depending on the severity of the circumstances. The employee shall have the opportunity to file a rebuttal if he or she does not agree with the contents of the written warning, suspension or discharge.

Several attempts shall be made by the administration to correct deficiencies before termination becomes necessary. Any written warning will only be in effect for one calendar year from the date on that notice. No employee shall be verbally reprimanded in front of students, parents or other personnel. Professional courtesy dictates that reprimands are to be conducted in private.

Most professionals would surely agree that employee discipline should be applied fairly and that some unacceptable conduct is remediable. They would also probably agree that some unacceptable conduct is not remediable and should not, therefore, be subjected to progressive discipline.

Egregious acts, such as fighting, theft or gross disobedience, may well be treated as irremediable and subject to a good deal more than an oral reprimand, including dismissal in some cases.[2]

> **UNION PROPOSAL** — *When an employee is required to appear before the administration or the board of education the employee shall be entitled to have a union representative present, if one is requested.*

It is good practice to allow union representation at conferences when discipline is contemplated – oral reprimands, written warnings, suspensions, or termination of employment. The very broad language of this proposal, however, allows for representation at any time the administration requests a meeting, including evaluation conferences or when a principal simply wants to investigate a fight between two students in a teacher's classroom. For some meetings, presence of a union representative may well be considered inappropriate or even a violation of a student's rights.

> **UNION PROPOSAL** — *Teachers shall be informed of all parental complaints. Parents will be required to meet with the teacher regarding any complaints. Prior to any discipline because of a parent complaint, the board or administration shall have a meeting with the teacher.*

School officials cannot guarantee that a parent will agree to meet with a teacher. The collective bargaining agreement is an agreement between the union and the school board. Any other persons or organizations should not be addressed in the agreement.

Employee Evaluation

> **UNION PROPOSAL** — *Non-tenured teachers shall be evaluated at least three times in each school year.*

---

[2] Case law in Illinois clearly distinguishes conduct that is remediable from that which is not.

Tenured teachers shall be evaluated at least once a year.

Evaluating all non-tenured teachers at least three times a year sounds good. In reality, however, very few school districts have the administrative resources necessary to complete that many evaluations. State law requires that tenured teachers be evaluated at least once every two years.

UNION PROPOSAL — *The supervisor shall acquaint each employee with the evaluation procedures, criteria and evaluation form to be used. No formal evaluations may take place until such orientation has been completed.*

This is an example of contract language that sounds like harmless common sense. However, such provisions subject virtually every administrative task to the grievance procedure. Overlooking even a minor aspect of the evaluation procedure becomes a contract violation. The school board should ask itself whether the teacher union contract is an appropriate place for administrator job descriptions.

UNION PROPOSAL — *The administration shall evaluate each teacher in writing using an evaluation instrument designed by the union and the administration and shall provide a copy of said evaluation to each teacher. Each formal evaluation shall include an in-class observation of the teacher's performance.*

If the school board believes that the supervision of employees is the responsibility of management, then the evaluation instrument should be designed by the administration — not the union. And keep in mind that making evaluation subject to the union contract also makes any procedural violations or adverse ratings of a teacher subject to the grievance procedure.

UNION PROPOSAL — *The evaluator shall have a post conference with the employee within five working days following the formal evaluation observation of* *the teacher. The employee shall have the right to challenge any adverse ratings listed on the evaluation instrument.*

Few if any school districts have the administrative staff necessary to provide a post conference within five days of the formal observation. Moreover, where any teacher is allowed to challenge any adverse rating, the principal will likely be fearful of open and honest comments.

Again, allowing such a provision in the contract will probably lead to contract violations and unnecessary grievances.

UNION PROPOSAL — *In all instances, evaluation procedures for all staff shall be conducted in conformance with the district evaluation plan jointly developed by the union and the administration.*

Again, input should advisably be obtained from the union, but responsibility for the final evaluation plan should rest with the board and administration.

Reduction in Force

Most teacher union contracts in Illinois probably contain some language regulating staff reductions — or layoffs. Although the Illinois School Code sets legal requirements for reductions in force (RIF), the statute[3] is silent on some aspects of staff reduction and it is in the interests of both board and union to clarify those matters. In addition, the law allows the school board and union to provide their own method for determining the sequence of dismissals.

In the Tenth Edition of *Illinois School Law Survey* (2008), author Brian Braun summarizes the Illinois law this way:

"A school board contemplating a reduction in teaching force must first remove or dismiss all non-tenured teachers in a particular position before removing or dismissing any tenured teacher who is legally qualified to hold the position.

---

[3] 105 ILCS 5/24-12

"As between tenured teachers, the teacher with the shorter length of continuous service to the district must be dismissed first unless an alternative method of determining the sequence of dismissal is established in a collective bargaining agreement.

"A school board must comply with all procedures required by its collective bargaining agreement in conducting a reduction in force."

Because the law does not address some key issues in staff reduction, the school board should seek some well-crafted clarifications. Competent legal guidance is essential in drafting such language, but in general terms the board should seek language that, among other things:

• specifies the maximum amount of time that a teacher has for exercising recall rights;

• makes each individual teacher responsible for providing the district with current certification information to ensure accurate placement on a seniority list.

Unions, on the other hand, will seek to make staff reductions as difficult as possible. The object, of course, is to prevent layoffs. For example:

UNION PROPOSAL — *The school board may reduce staff only when there has been a substantial reduction in state and local monies. The board shall first remove or dismiss all probationary teachers before dismissing tenured teachers.*

A board may wonder what exactly is meant by "substantial reduction." The board also might wonder why the district should lay off a probationary chemistry teacher when the aim is to eliminate a teaching position in English. (Illinois law limits bumping rights to teachers who are qualified to hold a position. The union proposal ignores that limitation.)

The real issue is whether it would be good public policy for the board to surrender its right to determine staff size.

Other union proposals typically seek to grant seniority rights to non-tenured teachers and extend recall rights to two years (one year is provided in the statute). Again, these proposals limit the ability of the board and administration to make staffing decisions and should be evaluated with the help of legal counsel.

Other Typical Proposals

UNION PROPOSAL — *When a vacancy arises, the superintendent or designee shall post such vacancy notices in all teachers' lounges for at least two weeks.*

As a courtesy to an individual employee, the board shall mail individual vacancy notices to the employee's home address during the summer months.

Current employees shall be given primary consideration for all vacancies of the district if qualified. In the case of equal qualifications the most senior teacher shall be given preference.

Here are some problems with these provisions:

• The ability of school administrators to fill jobs with the most qualified candidates should not be compromised by language in the collective bargaining agreement.

• Sending vacancy notices to an employee during the summer months is both time consuming and costly.

• Giving primary consideration to current employees or giving the position to the most senior applicant among employees with equal qualifications are requirements that invite both ill will and formal grievances.

Again, the discretionary authority of the board and administration need not and should not be restricted by collective bargaining language. Current employees can be notified and encouraged to apply. They can then compete for job openings on an equal basis with non-employees.

UNION PROPOSAL — *All terms and conditions of employment, including wages, hours of work, extra compensation for duties outside regular work hours, relief periods, leaves, and general employment condi-*

tions of all bargaining unit members / positions shall be maintained at not less than the highest minimum standards in effect for such bargaining unit member/position at the time this agreement is signed.

Applicable law in Illinois requires school boards to bargain with employee unions over the impact of changes that affect working conditions. The above proposal goes further and requires the board to get union approval of the change itself, not merely the impact.

For example, the maintenance of standards clause requires the board to get union approval in order to reduce staff, reduce the number of co-curricular activities, change the number of periods in a school day, change teaching assignments and the like.

UNION PROPOSAL — *The existing policies and procedures of the school district are hereby incorporated into this agreement, provided these policies and procedures may neither countermand nor be contrary to the other terms and conditions of this agreement.*

This clause makes all school board policies and administrative rules subject to the grievance procedure and binding arbitration. Further, any changes to those policies or rules require union assent.

UNION PROPOSAL — *The employment year for all full-time teachers shall not exceed 176 pupil attendance days and four institute days. The salary schedule shall be based on the maximum calendar of 180 days. Prior to adoption of the calendar by the board, the board and the union will meet and mutually agree to the school calendar for the following school year.*

By law, adoption of the school calendar is the exclusive duty of the board of education. Moreover, there may be years when the board cannot limit the work year to 180 days.

Unless the board wishes to give the union an equal voice

in establishing the school calendar, this clause should not be allowed in the contract. Rather, the board should seek the union's input but retain for itself the final decision regarding the calendar.

> **UNION PROPOSAL** — *The parties agree that applicable Illinois statutes and case law and the Constitution of the United States and the state of Illinois are hereby incorporated into this agreement.*

This clause makes all laws — constitutional, statutory and judicial — subject to the grievance procedure and subject to arbitration. Both the union and the individual employee already have access to the courts for alleging violations of these laws. This clause gives them a second avenue of appeal with access to an arbitrator and gives the arbitrator the authority to interpret all laws.

The proper review should be through the judicial system and not through an administrative law judge (arbitrator).

Finally, be sure to keep in mind that it is very costly to litigate the interpretation of language in a collective bargaining agreement. Be cautious in examining proposed contract language. With "status quo" requirements, any language included in the collective bargaining agreement may be impossible to delete or modify without expensive trade-offs.

INDEX

---

n = footnote

Contracts
defined, 94
distinction between policies and, 33–34
expansion of statutory procedures by, 22
goal of teacher unions in bargaining of, 32–33
pitfalls in, 102–113
Counterproposals of school board, 24–25
Court injunction in breaking strike, 77
Craft employee, 84
Credibility
building, 51
importance of, 50
Crisis bargaining, 94

- D -

Decertification of bargaining unit, 94
Decisional bargaining, 13, 35, 36, 37
Decision making, site-based, 41
Defacto bargaining, 4
Disputes, 66–71
arbitration of, 68–69
defined, 94
fact-finding in, 67–68
grievances and grievance procedures in, 69–70, 112
impasse in, 66–67
mediation of, 67
non-striking employees and, 77–78
right to strike, 70–71
unfair labor practices and, 7–8
Dock days, 75–76
Dues check-off, 94
Duty to bargain, 85–86

- E -

Early retirement plans, 104
Emotional issues, creation of, in school bargaining, 9
Employee bargaining units in school districts, 2–3
Employee relations, distinguishing between labor relations and, 15
Employees
confidential, 84, 93
coverage of, in Illinois Educational Labor Relations Act, 83–84
craft, 84
discipline of, 104–107

- S -

Other books published by the Illinois Association of School Boards

Visit www.iasb.com/shop/ to learn more about these and dozens of other books available from the Illinois Association of School Boards.

Illinois School Law Survey — Here are hundreds of legal questions and answers based on state and federal statutes, administrative rules and court decisions. Quick Reference Index and a searchable CD ROM make it easy to find the right answers. Updated and published in a new edition every other year.

Coming to Order — A Guide to Successful School Board Meetings — This book explains how to plan and conduct meetings that serve the interests of both school and community. Aimed at both new and experienced board members, the book should be especially useful to board presidents, secretaries and superintendents.

Essentials of Illinois School Finance — This book is both a training manual and desk-top reference for school business mangers and budget makers and anyone else who wants to understand the essentials of Illinois school finance. Covers everything from the peculiarities of property taxes and state funding to the formulas for projecting enrollments and staffing budgets. A revised edition is published every other year.

The School Official's Guide to Student Disciplinary Hearings — This step-by-step guide reviews the law governing student suspensions and expulsions in Illinois and provides detailed suggestions for organizing and conducting suspension/expulsion hearings. Explains different roles of administrators, hearing officers, school boards and attorneys.

For more information, contact:

IASB PUBLICATIONS
2921 Baker Drive
Springfield, Illinois 62703-5929
217/528-9688, extension 1108

www.iasb.com